postscripts

postscripts

Retrospections on Time and Place   Robert Root

UNIVERSITY OF NEBRASKA PRESS   LINCOLN & LONDON

© 2012 by the Board of Regents of the
University of Nebraska

Acknowledgments for the use of copyrighted
material appear on page ix, which constitutes
an extension of the copyright page.

Manufactured in the United States of America

⊚

Library of Congress Cataloging-in-Publication
Data

Root, Robert L.
Postscripts : retrospections on time and place /
Robert Root.
p. cm.
Includes bibliographical references.
ISBN 978-0-8032-3846-6 (pbk.: alk. paper)
1. Place (Philosophy) 2. Time (Philosophy)
3. Root, Robert L—Travel. 4. Root, Robert L—
Homes and haunts. 5. College teachers—
Biography. I. Title.
BIO5.P53R66 2012
814'.54—dc23
2012001111

Set in Scala.

For Zola,
who raised the level of my perception,
and for Ezra, Louie, Lilly, and Eliza,
who keep it high
—with love

I tend to write about events or circumstances
that raise the level of my perception.

—E. B. WHITE

In my walks I would fain return to my senses.
What business have I in the woods, if I am
thinking of something out of the woods?

—HENRY DAVID THOREAU

contents

acknowledgments

For those essays that have been published earlier, usually in a somewhat different form, I am grateful to these publications:

Ascent for "Knowing Where You've Been" and "Time and Tide"

Colorado Review for "Terra Cognita"

The Concord Saunterer for "The Everlastingly Great Look of the Sky: Thoreau and E. B. White at Walden Pond"

divide for "Here Is New York"

Ecotone: Reimagining Place for "The Pattern of Life Indelible"

North Dakota Quarterly for "Anasazi"

The Pinch for "Postscript to a Postscript to 'The Ring of Time'"

Rivendell for "Words in the Wind"

The River Review / Revue Riviere for "To Think of Time"

Under the Sun for "Shore Lines"

I am also grateful to editors W. Scott Olsen, Stephanie G'Schwind, Richard N. Schneider, Kristen Iversen, Steven Wingate, David Gessner, Robert W. Lewis, Sebastian Matthews, and Heidemarie Z. Weidner; the College of Humanities and Social and Behavioral Sciences at Central Michigan University; the Bread Loaf Writers' Conference; the Teller Wildlife Refuge and the Environmental Writing Institute; and the Artist-in-Residence Program at Acadia National Park. *Gratitude* is an insufficient word to describe my feelings at living a life as husband to Sue; father to Tom, Caroline, and Becky; father-in-law to Tim and Paul; and grandfather to Zola, Ezra, Louie, Lilly, and Eliza.

prologue

Words in the Wind
(The Green Mountains, Vermont)

In the aerial photograph on the postcard, Bread Loaf's oval campus dominates the foreground, and the unbroken deep green blur of the surrounding mountains throws its features—vibrant yellow meeting halls and lodgings, stark white library and theater, expansive light green lawns—into bright contrast. The encircling forest casts the viewer's gaze back toward the campus whenever it strays from it. This place must be the center of things, the viewer thinks, and doesn't wonder how far that forest extends beyond the edges of the postcard or what it conceals.

We who attend the writers' conference here get to live for a week in that postcard. Returning from a brief exploratory walk through the field across the road, down to a little river whose gurgling current sounds like unintelligible conversation, I seem to enter the establishing shot of a campus movie. The mown path arches uphill, and at first I seem to stroll toward sky, then, farther up the path, toward the tips of distant mountains. When I reach the level, I am facing the campus itself, which replaces both mountains and sky in my vision the closer I approach. Other workshoppers spread out across the porches and walks, appearing from a distance to be lively and earnest and thoroughly engaged with one another. Their words reach me in light gusts at first, then in a steady gale of sound as I cross the road. By the time I enter the main meetinghouse, a whirlwind of words has encircled me, and the mountains have disappeared from view.

Our days are measured by workshops, classes, performances, meetings, and meals, our inner lives exposed and explored in interior spaces; we move from room to room, building to building. Outdoors, when we slip off to read or write in the green and yellow Adirondack chairs scattered across the lawns, we usually face the campus, where our doppelgangers dodge among the buildings. We let the curious mountains look over our shoulders at the words on the pages that preoccupy our gaze. The hum of distant voices rises and falls with shifting breezes.

Talk is everywhere—we are not only writers and readers of words but performers of words, analyzers of words, generators of uncountable words about the words we've generated. In the dining hall the words rise to a din that bounces off the walls, like engines at a stock car race, and I leave each meal dazed and deafened.

Looking for a quiet place to discuss my manuscript, my workshop leader and I climb to the third-floor porch of the faculty rooming house, on the side out of the persistent wind. Our chairs face the mountains, but we look only at one another as we talk. He explains his creative process and examines my work-in-progress; I query, respond, and react. We watch each other form words, talk intently of art and artifice, soon hear only each other's words and not the wind.

I leave the porch trying to memorize his words in the hope that they will guide my revision, then rush to another porch, shaded and out of the way, on the side of the main meetinghouse. There I face an editor, enthroned in a corner, screened off by building walls and bushes rising above the porch railing. More words. She scans my written words in a proposal on her lap, and we exchange spoken words about them, mine earnest and expository and, I hope, persuasive, hers practical, efficient, authoritative, conveyed with a sympathetic (and gently discouraging) charm.

A friend here has told me that her goal in writing is "to be part of the conversation." When my second porch interview is over, I try to gauge my own place in that conversation by the measure of these interviews. I drift back to my room, replaying the meetings in my mind and listening for clues about my words. I find my workshop roommate stretched comfortably on his bed, reading. He asks what the weather's like outside. Even though I've been outdoors for over two hours, I am startled to have to tell him I don't know.

The next day I strike out for the mountains.

The trees lining the rough dirt road behind the Bread Loaf campus cut off my view at once. I drive slowly, raising a lethargic wake of dust, until I arrive at the parking area for the Skylight Pond Trail. It is midafternoon by the time I start walking. After I pass a few returning hikers near the trailhead, I am alone in the woods. The day is cool and the trail shaded by a thick canopy of maple and beech, but the walking warms me as I climb steadily from the trailhead. Soon I enter the Bread Loaf Wilderness, a portion of the Green Mountains National Forest. A posted map indicates boundaries and limits of spaces that can't be discerned on site, in the thick woods, on the dense forest floor. The woods offer no easy passage through, except on the trail itself and the occasional creek bed or storm wash that crosses it, and my range of vision is limited on every side. Hiking in shadow over uneven terrain, I concentrate on placing my footsteps, the words of the past several days echoing in my brain. I relive conversations, analyze advice, revise and compose and imagine, and trudge upward. Sun and sky break through the canopy only near the top of the mountain.

It is too late in the day, and I have come too unprepared to make a lengthy hike. At the intersection of the Skylight Pond Trail and the Long Trail, the one that crosses Vermont lengthwise from Massachusetts to Quebec, I shake off distractions and consider my options, then turn south toward the nearby peak of Battell Mountain. The top of the mountain is less crowded than the slopes but still lushly overgrown. Open spaces through the trees appear to promise unrestricted vision, but when I approach them, I quickly drop off the level, and the potential vista disappears behind barriers of treetops and dense thickets of young firs. A side path leads me to a small opening through the trees on the western slope and, just below it, to an outcropping of granite, large and bare. The sky is the only thing beyond it. I lower myself carefully to a ledge across from it, leap a deep, narrow crevice, and pull myself onto its slanting, uneven surface.

The peak of Battell Mountain is 3,482 feet. The outcropping is perhaps 100 feet lower. Exposed on the boulder, I feel the insistent strength of the wind. It quickly cools my sweat-dampened T-shirt and hair, tugs at my hat. I make every movement cautiously, deliberately. I take off my daypack, take out my binoculars, my daybook, and my pen; I position things so they will not slide away from me and plunge off the mountain, and I continually remind myself not to lunge after anything that does. Then I settle in and gaze across the terrain. The unobstructed view I have achieved is so expansive, its scale so vast, its horizons so distant, that I have to survey it slowly to take it all in.

I am at first aware only of ragged strips of green and blue, like randomly torn and variously shaded pieces of construction paper arranged in a layered collage—the dark green of fir and spruce sprinkled with stands of oak and beech immediately below me, the brighter green of the maple canopy lower down, the dull green of the mountains across the valley, the rich green of farmlands visible through the mountain gaps, and, in the hazy distance, more mountain chains, their colors changing from blue-green to shades of blue, growing lighter with each range. I shift my gaze slowly, overwhelmed and wordless. My mind empties of language and rallies all its resources to process sight, while the wind whispers past my ears, sotto voce, from the direction of my vision.

Many minutes pass uncounted before I attempt to recover the power of thought and try to identify what I see. At once I figure out that Bread Loaf Mountain is the higher peak looming nearby to the north. Then I realize that the line of distant mountains to the west, emerging from the haze where I mistook them for a low dark band of clouds, must be the Adirondacks, where I hiked just weeks ago. As if a closer view could confirm it, I lift my binoculars to scan them, then recognize the long irregular pale blue strip puddled before them as Lake Champlain. Unsure of my position on the outcropping, I feel nonetheless well grounded in my location.

I begin to search the nearer landscape for particulars, beginning with a glinting in the forest that catches my eye, a large pond in the middle of a forest clearing. Through field glasses I vainly search its marshy shallows for moose, then swivel toward another, longer pond farther south and inspect that as well. In the periphery of my vision I notice yet another clearing to the south and, when I swing toward it, recognize the campus of our conference. My position is behind and above the view on the postcard, beyond the northerly reaches of forest the photograph only suggests, higher and more distant. I steady my binoculars against my knee and scan the yellow buildings, picking out the barn, the inn, the faculty house. From here the library and the theater are hidden by trees, and the academics and artists are as invisible as moose. I focus on the porches of the faculty house, where yesterday I gazed complacently at this mountain. Now I gaze back from the mountain, serenely. Complacency is not the same as serenity.

I remember then how the postcard representation of the campus centered it in that panorama. From the mountain, though, the campus is merely a carefully maintained clearing, an artifice as deliberate and artful as the setting in a novel or a poem. Off to one side and hard to notice except for its size, it is less integrated with the landscape than the forest ponds I see gleaming in the distance.

I become aware of how silent it is, how silent I have been. Sitting on that outcropping, shaking in the wind, cooled and unsettled by its force and the precariousness of my perch, I close my eyes to center myself on listening. The landscape vanishes, the campus vanishes, the granite vanishes. I hear only the wind, emptied of all other sound, carrying only its own voice, and I vibrate sympathetically, like a tuning fork.

Somehow the wind has drawn me into the conversation that the universe carries on with itself, without ceasing. I open my eyes slowly, in order to keep my balance, and before I have to begin my descent, I listen a while longer to the solitary voice of the wind.

(The Green Mountains, Vermont)

one

To Think of Time
(The Habitation, Nova Scotia)

To think of time—of all that retrospection,
To think of today, and the ages continued henceforward . . .
To think that the sun rose in the east—that men and women were flexible,
    real, alive—that everything was alive,
To think that you and I did not see, feel, think, nor bear our part,
To think that we are now here and bear our part.
—WALT WHITMAN, "To Think of Time"

On the morning after the night the old millennium ended, I rose groggily a little after eight, shuffled bleary-eyed to the bedroom window, and brushed aside the curtain. Blinking back the fog of sleep, I peered outside. The remnants of my life span would cover only a minuscule portion of this new millennium. I wanted a glimpse of it before stumbling downstairs to start living through its brief early scenes and my (hopefully long) final act.

In our front yard, where the north side of the house shields the ground from the winter sun, the mottled remnants of the second millennium's final snowfall lay patchy and stuccoed with late leaves from its final autumn. Away from the shadow of our house the ground was bare and dry, its snow removed by sun and wind over the last week. The sky was clear and pale blue. The weather had not altered overnight with the new millennium. The year 2000 had arrived on the International Dateline at 6 a.m. Eastern Standard Time, passed through the midnights of seventeen intervening time zones while we waited our turn to welcome the future, and moved west beyond us for six hours more. By the time I awoke on New Year's Day most parts of the world were already on their second day in the third millennium, but from my window at least, the twentieth century and the twenty-first century seemed identical.

As my vision cleared I gazed up and down our block. None of the other houses showed signs of life. The nonagenarian across the way was no doubt spending New Year's Day at her daughter's house, and the fraternity houses and student rentals were still empty over the college's inter-semester recess. One car cruised slowly north on Maple Street but even the neighborhood squirrels seemed to be sleeping in. I saw no sign of the third millennium, no indication even that it was Saturday, and early January was indistinguishable from late December.

Downstairs Sue had let the dog out and let her back in, made coffee, and started working at her place at the dining room table. The dog had successfully completed her morning migration from her upstairs bed to her downstairs bed and looked at me disinterestedly, shifting her gaze without moving her head. In the living room three transparent star-shaped helium balloons decorated with gold stars, New Year's Eve mementos, swayed on ribbons tied to a foil-wrapped conical anchor stone. Only the balloons made the day seem different from any other.

We'd seen the New Year in at the home of friends and stayed on chatting over a background of television commentary. In Times Square, while cheering people still crowded together in y2k hats or year 2000 glasses or blue and gold foil wigs, news personalities began reporting the failure of things to fail; despite their best efforts, they had found nothing going wrong. They seem discouraged. Sam Donaldson, importantly stationed at the "y2k Command Center," according to the caption on the screen, observed, "The real news is, there is no news." Lisa Stark, a lesser luminary covering mere Washington, soon after reported, "The real story is, there is no story." There being no news and no story didn't prevent the millennial anchorperson and the reporters from opining at length about nonevents and the importance of the media in regard to them, but the real significance of the conversation was, there was no significance.

One of our friends observed that the problem with media coverage of the millennium was that it wasn't covering events or people; it was covering time itself, and there was nothing to show. (The event was, there was no event.) The clock ticked, the big hand moved $\frac{1}{60}$th of a circle, the visual event was over. In Times Square a massive Waterford crystal ball plummeted slowly to light up a 2000 sign, but that was just a flashy tick of the clock. The fireworks and the confetti and the cheering throng were not the tick but the aftermath of the tick, no more significant than the empty street I awoke to this morning.

I remember once having thought, perhaps in 1950, when the twentieth century was halfway through, that I'd probably never see the year 2000. The end of the century was so far away, so out of reach. But it wasn't far; it didn't take long to reach it at all. We talk of dates and events as milestones, a measure of space metaphorically indicating a measure of time, but milestones only indicate distance between one terminus and another—they are not the destination. In space they're useful as measures of how far we've come and how far we have to go; in time they measure nothing at all. What does this "milestone," the end of the second millennium of the Christian era, mean to the planet? to the solar system? to the galaxy? to the universe? Has the big hand landed on 12 for the universe, or has only the second hand twitched? (Never mind the question of Chinese and Jewish and Muslim and Hindu calendars; never mind the problem that the millennial celebration should have come at the end of 2000, not the beginning.)

On New Year's Eve 1999, early in around-the-world coverage of the New Year, I saw revelers in Antarctica being interviewed. They announced how hard they were going to party, how much they hoped people back home would be partying, how concerned they were about the Wildcats' (or maybe Bobcats' or Tigercats') big game on New Year's Day. They sounded, in other words, exactly like the revelers in Akron or Albany or Altoona. The significance of their being in Antarctica was, it had no significance. None in space, apparently, since location altered nothing about their behavior, and certainly none in time.

"To think of time—of all that retrospection," Whitman mused. "To think of today, and the ages continued henceforward." In my study I pulled open the curtains of the window behind the computer and could not find the millennium in the backyard either. But I didn't really expect to and instead turned away from the window, to a folder of old travel notes, trying to think my way back to one of the places where I felt I had encountered time.

On a morning in mid-June 1995 we check out of a bed-and-breakfast in Digby, Nova Scotia, and begin the drive around Annapolis Basin to Port Royal. The basin, an inlet of the Bay of Fundy, is foot shaped. Digby nestles at the heel, the basin stretches northeast like a long thin instep, and the highway parallels the sole. All along the highway wild lupine blooms, in pinks and blues and purples, bright against brown grasses. At the end of the foot we circle around the toes, cross the Annapolis River and pass through the town of Annapolis Royal, then double back along the upper side of the foot, looking for the reconstruction of the Habitation at Port Royal National Historic Site.

The Habitation is a notable site in North American history. This is the first place north of the Caribbean that Europeans attempted to establish a permanent base in North America. The European settlement of Canada began here. In little over a hundred years after Columbus made contact with the New World, the French had established a presence in the northern latitudes, where they hoped to locate a northwest passage around the New World to Asia. Expeditions by John Cabot and Samuel de Champlain had already pressed on up the St. Lawrence River from the Gulf of St. Lawrence. In the early years of the seventeenth century Pierre du Gua, Sieur de Monts, was granted a trading monopoly by the French king, Henri iv, with the stipulation that, in addition to building a permanent trading post, he establish a colony in Nouvelle France. In 1604 colonists, de Monts and Champlain among them, attempted to maintain themselves in the Bay of Fundy on Ste. Croix Island, a small island with limited resources; half of them died of starvation and scurvy over a harsh winter. In 1605 they relocated to the site of Port Royal, on the mainland of what the French would identify as l'Acadie, or Acadia, and what would later be called Nova Scotia.

The area around the reconstructed Habitation is now well populated, particularly on the road near Annapolis Royal, and the landscape of private homes and small businesses and farms is unremarkable, a scene that could be observed with slight variations of terrain across late-twentieth-century North America. We could be driving between the city where we live and any number of neighboring communities in mid-Michigan. It's the Habitation, when we reach it, that reminds us where we are, not only on the map but also in time.

The site occupies a small space between the highway and the basin. The parking lot is small, and a grove of trees blocks off the view of the Habitation until we emerge from them and see the outer walls, a plain facade of dark gray, rough, weathered boards. We circle the exterior toward the basin, where an upright defensive palisade extends out from the main entrance. Across from the palisade, at the other end of the buildings, a cannon platform similarly juts out from the main structure, to allow defenders to catch attackers from the basin in a cross fire. We enter through the recessed entrance and find ourselves in a flat grassy inner square surrounded by steeply roofed buildings, all abutting one another tightly though varied in height and breadth. In the center of the square, where stone walks from each of the four walls meet to form a cross, is a well with a fieldstone wall and a small roof. In the grassy sections between the walks and the buildings are signs of daily labor: two tubs and a washboard in one rectangle, a barrel and a handcart in another, in a third the shavings-strewn workplace of the woodwright with its sawhorses, fresh cut timber, and tools.

We investigate the interiors of the buildings in a clockwise tour: the forge, the kitchen, the bakery, the artisans' quarters, the chapel, gentlemen's dwellings, the residence of the company's chief officers, the storeroom, the sail loft, the trading room, the guard room. All of the rooms that are open for inspection are sparsely equipped with furniture and implements made on the scene, using reconstructed tools of the period. The effect is to give the site a sense of newness, of recent construction. The authenticity is in the details.

I've visited many forts and historic buildings over the years and have always been conscious of the extent to which they have been reconstructed or revived. It's difficult to maintain buildings intact over centuries when they have been abandoned or neglected, as so many fortresses have been. Stone walls crumble, wooden buildings weather and collapse, nature reclaims any place without persistent preservation efforts. In some historic buildings the sense of authenticity comes from recovered original furnishings of the period—the actual desk that such and such a writer used, the actual cradle that such and such a statesman's infant children slept in, the silverware of a pattern used in the period by a different family in the same region. Or it comes from replicating known aspects of the building— a painting that copies an original portrait of a contemporary of the people who lived in the house, wallpaper specially manufactured to duplicate a design popular in the period, a chair upholstered to match the fabric in a photo of the homeowner late in life. It's something to be in the presence of artifacts that historical figures have used and touched, to feel you are occupying the same space that they moved through, as though they had stepped out just before you stepped in. It's one way to be transported in time, and it has the benefit of keeping you constantly aware of the passage of time. The age and condition of an artifact or a structure makes it venerable in your mind, in addition to whatever reverence you might feel for the cultural icon who lived there or the circumstances of the lives of people of the period.

Of necessity the Habitation transports you in time a different way. It closes the gap between then and now by treating *then* as if it were *now*. It was never venerable but always vital. Though the reconstruction has now survived longer than the original did, in its time the Habitation seemed similarly this recent. Its timbers were hewn on the spot, its furnishings manufactured on site by colony artisans, its walls just this rough to the touch, and the smell of wood shavings

To Think of Time

on the ground just this fresh and pungent. The colonists were just as stout and robust as these bearded young men in rough blouses and breeches and floppy toques bustling through their daily chores of reenactment. Four centuries ago none of this was historic; all of this was new. The reconstruction and reenactment collapses time, interlocks then and now, makes the past more immediate, and momentarily obscures your sense of the intervening centuries without obliterating it.

So. In the way that such historic sites often do, the Habitation at Port Royal helps us think of time by letting us temporarily bridge the gap of centuries. But as we tour the Habitation this day, I become aware of other connections, of feeling somehow that the bridge runs both ways and that the past is more than a casual visitor in the present.

The colony at the Habitation was short lived. The intricacies of the politics behind the occupation of the Habitation are well told in Elizabeth Jones's *Gentlemen and Jesuits* (1986), from which I draw the details of the following sketch of its history. The French established good relations with the Micmac people of the region (also identified as the Mi'kmaq or Souriquois) and their chief, Membertou. The Sieur de Monts, who had shared the hardships of the year on St. Croix, returned to France and remained there while Jean de Biencourt, Sieur de Poutrincourt, returned to the Habitation with a new company of men. When de Monts lost his monopoly on the fur trade and Poutrincourt and the colonists were forced to sail back to France in 1607, Membertou and the Micmacs expected them to return and made certain the Habitation remained intact and well preserved over the interval. De Monts's attention was increasingly drawn to the interior of Canada, toward Quebec, but Poutrincourt struggled to reestablish the settlement at Port Royal. In 1610 Poutrincourt, his son Charles de Biencourt, and a company of settlers and Jesuit missionaries returned to the Habitation and restored relations with the Micmacs. Despite tension between the Protestant Poutrincourt, who wanted to build a permanent settlement at Port Royal, and the zealous Catholic missionaries, who wanted to convert the Micmac to Christianity at almost any cost, the settlers at the Habitation thrived and lived in neighborly harmony with the Micmacs. But international politics took a hand in affairs. In 1613, in one of the earliest acts that marked the conflict between France and England for control of eastern North America—a conflict that would not be resolved until France's loss of Nouvelle France at the Treaty of Paris in 1763 and which still simmers in the Quebec separatist movement of the twentieth century—a group of English settlers from Virginia sailed north and burned the Habitation to the ground while all of its inhabitants were gone working in distant fields.

That was the end of the Habitation. The survivors found their mill still intact and set up living quarters there, but their provisions were not sufficient, and there was considerable hardship throughout the winter. Undoubtedly, Membertou and the Micmacs contributed to their well-being in some way, but when Poutrincourt arrived from France to inspect his settlement, he found all in ruins. Poutrincourt returned to France, but his son, Biencourt, stayed on, continuing to trade with the Micmac and living a life more similar to their lifestyle than to a European one. Intermarriage between the French and the Micmac helped to blur distinctions. The Habitation did not rise again until the replica was constructed in 1939 for the Port Royal National Historic Site.

As we tour the replica early in the tourist season, we are almost the only visitors. The reenactors go about their chores but don't need to perform for us. Instead, we rely on the attentions of a guide, Judy Pearson, dressed not in period costume but in a jaunty blue expedition hat and park ranger costume. In one of the dwellings she explains the symbols on a ceremonial moose hide cloak, pointing to the picture of a moose and depictions of caribou, herons, and longhouses. She says that the two young men outside dressed as seventeenth-century French artisans are in fact descendants of French colonists. She herself is Micmac, and members of her tribe, descendants of Membertou and his followers, still live throughout the region. To me it seems fitting that this knowledgeable woman putting us in touch with the Habitation's past is herself a descendant of the native people who first befriended the Europeans. The past here is not separated from the present; it is not merely a local curio or a disembodied theme park; it is still a portion of the time in which they are bearing their parts.

Much of what we know of the Habitation comes from the writing of Marc Lescarbot, a lawyer who spent a single year in Port Royal, from July 1606 to July 1607, but whose *Histoire de la Nouvelle France*, originally published in 1609 but revised and expanded in 1617 and 1619, covers events thoroughly. At the restored Habitation one of the dwellings is made up to look like one he might have lived in. The fascinating aspect of Lescarbot for me is his literary aspirations. He wrote a number of poems at the Habitation and created the first theatrical spectacle performed in the New World. As a graduate student twenty years earlier, I uncovered a reference to Lescarbot's *Le Théâtre de Neptune* in a history of French theater when I was reading medieval, Renaissance, and neoclassical French and English drama. I was then fascinated by court masques, particularly those of Ben Jonson, and began pursuing a literary tangent for the sheer delight in the chase. I once even considered writing a fresh translation of Lescarbot's play and still have a photocopy of the French text in my files. For two decades I had wanted to visit the Habitation.

Le Théâtre de Neptune is an intriguing artifact, drawing on both the court masque, in which courtiers acted out or danced allegorical roles usually drawn from classical mythology, and the civic *entrée*, or entry, a festive event welcoming royalty or nobility to a city with pageantry, theatrics, and feasting. Poutrincourt and Champlain had been away from the Habitation on an expedition of exploration since early September 1606, and when they arrived at Port Royal on November 14, they were greeted by a spectacle written, produced, and directed by Lescarbot.

Especially considering the wilderness circumstances, it was an elaborate performance. As Poutrincourt prepared to come ashore, he was greeted by Frenchmen in small boats dressed as Neptune, god of the sea, and six Tritons. Neptune, adorned in theatrical buskins, a blue veil, and a flowing beard and wig and holding a trident, hailed him as "Sagamos," the Micmac word for "chief," congratulated him on his valor, and extolled the triumph of France in the New World. Each of the six Tritons, except for one who spoke in a comic Gascon accent, enlarged upon that theme. Then a canoe with four Frenchmen garbed as New World Indians welcomed Poutrincourt, and the assembled group burst into a four-part song. The party came ashore, the trumpet was sounded, the cannon was fired, and the basin echoed with celebration: "& semble à ce tonnere que Prosperine soit en travail d'enfant: ceci causé par la multiplicité des Echoz que les côtaux s'envoient les uns aux autres, lesquels durent plus d'un quart d'heure" ("it seemed like the thunder when Prosperina [the wife of Neptune] is in labor, caused by the multiple echoes that the coast sends itself one after another, which last more than a quarter hour"). The entrance to the Habitation was decorated with the coats of arms of the king of France, the Sieur de Monts, and the Sieur de Poutrincourt, and "un compagnon de gailliard humeur," a merry fellow, welcomed them to a banquet and invited them to empty their cups, sneeze away their "frost humors," and inhale the sweetest vapors of the feast.

Most commentators remark that *The Theatre of Neptune* is no great literary shakes but also acknowledge Lescarbot's ingenuity and energy in composing and producing the event, especially recruiting the community under his charge to pour its energies into this superfluous pageantry by creating costumes, memorizing lines, and decorating the fort and the canoes. Its achievement is more in the area of building morale than in creating theater. Champlain, a more experienced colonist than Lescarbot, having spent two winters in New France, may have taken a page from Lescarbot's book by soon after proposing the Ordre de Bon Temps (Order of Good Cheer), a revolving designation of each of the gentlemen in the company as master of the feast for a day, responsible for providing food for the day's dinner; it was a scheme, as Jones notes, that produced a friendly rivalry that kept them active and healthy during the ensuing winter. Schoolchildren in Nova Scotia still learn about Lescarbot's *Theatre of Neptune* and Champlain's Order of Good Cheer, and both serve as emblems of perseverance and joie de vivre in the provincial spirit.

But Lescarbot's *entrée* is not simply the Acadian equivalent of the first Thanksgiving in Massachusetts. Whether by intention or happenstance, Lescarbot wove together several strands of history in his production. As is common in the court masque and the *ballet de cour* and similar Renaissance pageants, the personages of the present are linked to an ancient, epic past, to the mythological machinery of *The Odyssey* and *The Aeneid*. Similarly, Camões, in his epic of Portuguese exploration, *The Lusiads*, involved Venus and Jupiter in the fate of Vasco de Gama's expeditions and made Mercury accompany him on his voyages. To his own classical commonplaces Lescarbot added the roles of Micmac characters, drawing no doubt on his own observations of their traditions and customs—they offer gifts of moose meat, beaver skins, *matachias* (quill or bead embroidery), and the promise of fish. The Fourth Indian, who has yet to catch his gift, asks for bread (*caraconas*) to share with his people. The Triton who speaks with a Gascon accent and the merry companion who sets them sneezing and drinking represent the immediate company of explorers. Classical literature, aboriginal tradition, and national custom all blend (lightly) in this production. And the Micmac themselves are part of the audience, observers of an unfamiliar but colorful and curious ritual. Lescarbot's little show in the harbor fascinates me, not simply because it attempts to connect the explorations of Champlain and Poutrincourt with classical myth but because the show is performed in full view of the Micmacs, who get the rare opportunity to see the Europeans displaying ancestral lore. There are complicated layers of intertextuality here.

As we tour the restored Habitation, I am aware that all is replica, that the authentic artifacts of Lescarbot's time there had long ago made their way into some *bibliothèque* or *musée* in France or crumbled into dust. Yet I still feel a stirring of connection to the site. My long-ago interest in French drama, in sixteenth- and seventeenth-century theater, led me to Lescarbot, and he in turn led me here. In that amorphous way in which what we read can become part of what we experience, *The Theatre of Neptune* and the Habitation somehow became part of my personal history. Perhaps merely being a tourist here would have been enough to connect me, but I feel all the more connected because of what I knew and imagined about the place in the past. Some things came together here once before, and visiting the site makes things come together again, connecting with the present moment as well.

All this is recollected in the tranquility of my study on a millennial morning. The recollection recaptures the moment incompletely, of course, and draws on photographs and journal entries and notes for details, but nonetheless it transports me across time. I travel back five years in a light hop and then four hundred years in a brisk bound and pause at the threshold of the time that altered with the construction of the Habitation. I am in awe of the prospect of "all that retrospection," and it makes me conscious, almost in spite of myself, of the "ages continued henceforward."

It's often difficult to escape the orbit of the immediate. Moment by moment we are hurled toward the future at such relentless and frenetic speed that we can barely perceive what's coming, let alone notice what's gone. It's hard to overcome the gravitational field of the here and now—the daily round of getting and spending that lays waste our hours, the attention to getting ahead or getting along or getting by. We hardly know how to ponder who we are, where we come from, why we're here. The past is another country, and our eyes are in the front of our heads, always looking forward, barely distracted by peripheral vision, seldom looking over our shoulders to see how far we've come.

When, in the Book of Genesis, Lot and his family are spared the destruction of the cities of Sodom and Gomorrah, they are ordered by an angel to flee without looking back. Lot's wife looks back, and she is turned into a pillar of salt, a punishment for her disobedience, I suppose. Whatever the Old Testament moral of the story is meant to be, I've never been satisfied with the tale. Are we to learn from it not to acknowledge mass destruction as long as we ourselves survive? Are we to suppose that looking back itself is the fatal misconduct, that we will be punished if we wonder what's become of where we've been? Are we to think that Lot, who blindly and obediently goes on, never looking back, is the admirable figure, Lot's unnamed wife the sinful one? Why shouldn't we think that Lot's later unforgivable sin—the drunken and incestuous impregnation of his daughters—is a punishment for refusing to acknowledge where he comes from and who he is? To me the story would make more sense if Lot is punished for his callousness and Lot's wife were rewarded for breaking the rules, if God could stay his hand again because he realizes that, in Kurt Vonnegut's words, "it's very human" to look back. Lot's wife is the one I learn from here, even if the pillar of salt she becomes is formed of her own tears. Vonnegut says of his novel *Slaughterhouse Five*, "This book is a failure and it had to be, because it was written by a pillar of salt." Yes, I say, this essay too.

So. A new century or a new millennium arrives (or doesn't yet arrive), and it hardly matters when we celebrate it because we are centered on a moment virtually devoid of context in itself. A few weeks later I will want to stay up, as I did on New Year's Eve, to see a total lunar eclipse, but the night is overcast where I live, and it's lightly snowing, and the sky doesn't clear until after the eclipse. I will have no more sense of the eclipse that cloudy night than I had of the millennium on a night that was perfectly clear.

But during my visit to the Habitation, and in my memory of that visit, I do have a sense of event, and I do think of time. Roughly four centuries have passed since the Habitation was constructed and destroyed, but it's not exactly lost in time. We have Lescarbot's texts; we have written accounts of the colony; we have a reconstruction that replicates the design of the Habitation, if not entirely its ambience. And we have the opportunity to intersect with history—of the Micmacs, of the French in Acadia, of the court masque and public pageantry, of our own personal lives. These histories intersect whenever we examine where we are in time and what the various levels of the past have been where we are in space.

Suddenly we get that sense of awareness that Whitman speaks of, where we struggle to think "that the sun rose in the east" without us, to think "that men and women were flexible, real, and alive" when we had no existence, to think that it's only for this moment that "you and I are now here and bear our part." This is the moment to recognize that, as Whitman says,

> the law of the past cannot be eluded,
> the law of the present and the future cannot be eluded,
> the law of the living cannot be eluded, it is eternal.

To bear our part is to observe and acknowledge this eternal law.

But a portion of bearing our part is also to record this moment in which cultural and environmental and literary and personal histories intersect and to leave it as an inexact milestone for those who will bear their part after us. Let them encounter this artifact and say, "Ah, there's where we were; oh, here's where we are." We don't need to depend on global coverage by media conglomerates to provide it. We need only be awake and alert to moments of intersection; we need only think of time with humility and grace. The real story is, you and I are here now and bear our part. The real news is, every moment is a milestone.

two

The Pattern of Life Indelible
(Belgrade Lakes, Maine)

A lake is the landscape's most beautiful and expressive feature. It is earth's eye; looking into which the beholder measures the depth of his own nature.

—HENRY DAVID THOREAU, *Walden*

i. Great Pond 2002

I am surprised when I reach the end of the road. Strolling casually through Bear Springs Camp, gazing at the backs of cabins and glimpsing Great Pond beyond them, I expected to find a footpath through the woods, some way to keep following the shoreline. But I see only thick woods and dense undergrowth straight ahead. Knowing I have to retrace my steps, I glance longingly toward the shoreline, but the cabins are close together, and I'm reluctant to walk between them to reach it, timid about blundering into someone's privacy. Two cars with New Jersey plates are parked under the trees behind the last cabin. Where I find cars I will likely find people in the cabin or on the porch or at the water's edge. Boats tied up to the docks in front of each cabin also suggest that people are still around, and even earlier, when I passed a cabin without cars, I heard a baby fussing inside. Finding no trail into the woods and no unobtrusive path to the shoreline, I turn back the way I came.

A dozen yards ahead a woman stands in the middle of the dirt road, looking at me. We passed each other only a moment or two earlier, her brief "Guh mawning" linking her to the Jersey plates and the last cabin. She waits as I amble toward her and, before I am very near, asks if I'm looking for someone. I say no, just wandering. She asks if I'm staying here, at Bear Springs Camp. This is inland Maine, where folks are relaxed and friendly, but she's from New Jersey and prudently curious about strangers in the neighborhood with no apparent reason for being there. I say, "No, I'm not, but I'm trying to decide if I'd like to stay here next year." This is true but not the whole truth—I don't want to explain that I want to write about the place and that I'm here now because sixty years earlier E. B. White wrote about his own summers on this lake—and I hope my genuine desire one day to be a renter reassures her.

During this exchange I come almost even with her. She turns, and we start walking slowly together, back toward the center of camp. She is a soft, auburn-haired, pale-skinned woman in a striped short-sleeve pullover and dark blue shorts and sandals; I guess that she is somewhere in her late forties, maybe early fifties. She encourages me to rent a cabin—"This is a great place and you would love it." I ask if she's stayed at the camp before.

It turns out that she has been coming every year for two decades. Her daughter is twenty-five, and "we've been coming since she's five." Many of the other families here this week are people she has known for years, including friends of her children whom they see only at the camp when these far-flung families turn up once a year to stay for the same week in the same cabins. She tells me it's nice to go up to meals (they're on the "American Plan" here, three communal meals a day) and sit at a big table with other campers—"It's like a big family gathering. You get to know people." She says, "At the end of the week, when we leave, we book the cabin for the next year." I wonder aloud if that's why it's so hard to reserve a cabin.

She explains that some people she's met here have been coming for thirty or forty years. The kids keep coming even after they grow up, and when one generation stops coming, the family still reserves a cabin and the next generation shows up with children of their own. "There's death, you know, and people divorce, and they get too old, but that's the only thing that opens up spots," she says. "The turn-

The Pattern of Life Indelible

over is small. If you really want to come, put your name on Peg's list, and when someone cancels, then you can get in."

She points me toward the main beach, which I claim to be looking for, and indicates Peg's office in the other direction. Then she smiles and waves and ambles off to meet a friend from another cabin. I look up the dirt road and see my car parked on the side of the blacktop road, opposite the large white building housing the office and the dining hall and the separate little building with the guest laundry. Earlier, to get to the cabins, I followed the dirt road down the slope, gradual, grassy, open, and took the right fork when the road neared the shoreline. I strolled behind the cabins, under hemlocks, spruces, birches, aspen, the woods close and overgrown and the underbrush too dense to tramp through. On the shaded dirt road campers from the cabins scuffing out in the opposite direction occasionally greeted me, and I tried to make my ambling match the easy, unhurried pace of the people I passed, the pace of the life in the camp.

The cabins varied little, from duplexes to single units, some exteriors sided with logs and others with planks but the roofs always sheet metal and the color of the cabin walls always a dark woodsy brown, freshly repainted. All the cabins had roofed porches and docks and a little bit of green space between the cabin and the lake. Trees that mostly shaded them from the sun on the lake side were tall and close by the cabins. On the western, landward side of the peninsula, where the woods were thick and usually dark, the cabins were invisible from the blacktop road and blocked from the sun in the afternoon. I thought that darkness must come early here, the sun disappearing behind the trees and the distant western hills long before it disappears from the sky.

I follow the road down to the beach, settle onto a clump of sandy grass under a tree, very near the water, and take my daybook and pen out of my fanny pack. A rivulet running through the camp, shaded near the shoreline and crossed by a little bridge, curves around in front of me and disappears under the plywood dock a few feet away. I've located myself out of the way of the swimming area, near a red plastic paddleboat. Beached sailboats, inflatable dinghies, and kayaks line the shore in one direction, and in the other direction I can see a yellow version of the paddleboat and beyond it a large yellow inner tube. Three aluminum rowboats with outboard motors, all bearing the Bear Springs Camp insignia, are tied up to the dock in front of me, and a low runabout with a huge Yamaha outboard is moored at the end. I try to blend in with the setting, appear to be an idler from one of the cabins rather than an intruder who hasn't paid for this view. Soon I disappear into the landscape, and the pattern of life in the center of the camp reveals itself all around me.

Three young girls stroll along the beach in front of me, pausing to try to break open a mussel with a stone. No luck. After the girls move on, three young black ducks pass me, two floating down the rivulet, one waddling on the sand near the lake. Neither preoccupied trio shows any interest in my presence.

In the swimming area two children play with scuba masks while a man videotapes them. Beyond him an older couple, both thick and white-haired, pull a blue cover over the hatch of their white speedboat. Out beyond the swimming area, on an anchored raft almost directly ahead of me, a slim, dark-haired, teenaged girl in a blue one-piece swimsuit shifts from sitting up and leaning back on her hands to lying down and bracing herself on her elbows. Two younger girls skim down the coast in a two-person kayak, working vigorously. A mother and her very young daughter enter the water, the woman dragging an inflated plastic lounge chair, the girl dragging a large yellow inflated octopus with a fixed smile. Two middle-aged men, gray and soft, and two younger men, tanned and lean, wade out from the beach and begin playing catch with a large floating dart, which, when they throw it just the right way, makes a ringing noise like a cell phone; perhaps it is a comforting or reassuring sound to some of the people playing. The mother and daughter return to the shore, both smiling, the octopus still wearing its goofy grin. Another black duck wanders toward me, honking all the way, gets within a foot and a half before

The Pattern of Life Indelible

turning back. Three docks away two people board a blocky pontoon boat, with an awning covering the rear half.

The sky is hazy, the air humid, but the wind is brisk and cooling despite its warmth. The camp curves around the shoreline, facing mostly east and southeast, near the base of the peninsula stretching south into Great Pond toward Jamaica Point. The haze obscures the distant shores of Great Pond—only the near shoreline appears as a vivid green. The islands in the lake, the eastern shore, the hills beyond, are lighter and lighter shades of blue. Pale blue sky breaks through the haze sometimes, but though the sun is high now, as it nears midday, the shadows are seldom sharp or well defined. It is supposed to rain today, but I see nothing moving in yet.

On most of the cabin porches beach towels, swimsuits, t-shirts and similar colorful summer wear hang drying in the breeze (though not often in the sun). I can see a porch across the clearing where red, white, yellow, blue, and green strips of cloth are draped on the railing, pennants signaling family presence to those offshore. In the other direction the cabin three docks over has a clothesline on the far end of the porch, white plastic chairs and table taking up most of the floor space, and a pile of bright plastic inflatable water toys—rafts, dinghies, octopus, floating lounge chair—piled against the wall.

The men in the swimming area pursue their dart-catching game as far out as the raft and then end it to paddle around some and chat as they drift toward shore. In the distance I can hear the sound of Jet Skis—one is hurtling through the water towing a raft with someone lying prone hanging on to it. The runabout at the end of the near dock has gone out near a double kayak, and someone leaps from the boat and joins another young man in the kayak. On shore some people sit in a circle, slumped in white plastic chairs, conversing. In the distance I see a group of laughing women in lounge chairs and another group chatting on the cabin steps.

Peace and goodness and jollity, White called it, summertime, oh, summertime, pattern of life indelible. The only urgency is in the Jet Skis, and urgency is their nature, their reason for being—who rides a Jet Ski to be leisurely with their leisure time? Even the two men in the double kayak are being towed by the runabout, defeating the point of kayaking, I would guess. And yet it's all to pass the time, to do little that requires doing, to rest in between bouts of playing and relaxing and socializing, to feel that even urgency here is a form of play when it shows up.

As noon approaches and the sky hazes over more, the beach empties. I notice an osprey hovering above the lake and follow him with field glasses as he glides toward the peninsula, coming to rest on a high branch of a tree along the shore. From time to time I check to see if he too will join the activity on the lake. Except for the black ducks and chickadees calling in the distance and an occasional swallow darting out over the water, I haven't seen any other bird activity. Surely there are more birds in all this bug-filled forest. Then the osprey is gone and takes with him my sudden interest in bird-watching. I rise creakily after two hours in one cross-legged position and limber up slowly. As I follow the dirt road up the slope, I notice that the building where the campers gather for the midday meal is busy and the cabins behind me are quiet. Knowing that I'm going to my car instead of a communal meal makes me again aware that I am an outsider at Bear Springs Camp. But then why, I wonder, do I feel so comfortable here?

ii. Once More to the Lake 1941

E. B. White was someone who came often to Great Pond. As he says in the opening of his essay "Once More to the Lake": "One summer, along about 1904, my father rented a camp on a lake in Maine and took us all there for the month of August. We all got ringworm from some kittens and had to rub Pond's Extract on our arms and legs night and morning, and my father rolled over in a canoe with all his clothes on; but outside of that the vacation was a success, and from then on none of us ever thought there was a place in the world like that lake in Maine." His account of his first visit reads with the breathlessness of a child eager to get in everything in one telling,

The Pattern of Life Indelible

but as the essay progresses, he reveals that he is writing now about a visit to the pond he made with his own son and how finding himself in the role of father in a place where he was accustomed to the role of son confused him about the immediacy of the past and the present. It seems to him that he is reliving his own childhood rather than simply witnessing his son's experience of the camp—"I seemed to be living a dual existence. I would be in the middle of some simple act, I would be picking up a bait box or laying down a table fork, or I would be saying something, and suddenly it would be not I but my father who was saying the words or making the gesture. It gave me a creepy sensation." He sees a dragonfly alight on the tip of his fishing rod. "It was the arrival of this fly that convinced me beyond any doubt that everything was as it had always been, that the years were a mirage and there had been no years." Everything he sees around him he feels he has seen before, and when he dislodges the dragonfly as he had in childhood, he repeats himself: "There had been no years between the ducking of this dragonfly and the other one—the one that was part of memory." He sees one of the campers in the water with a cake of soap, "and the water felt thin and clear and unsubstantial. Over the years there had been this person with the cake of soap, this cultist, and here he was. There had been no years."

The changes White does observe and record are seemingly slight—the old three-track dirt road of the horse-drawn wagons is now a two-track of automobiles; the waitresses in the farmhouse dining room have cleaner hair, like girls in movies; there are louder, larger motors on the boats and more Coca-Cola, less sarsaparilla, birch beer, and Moxie in the little general store—but nonetheless they indicate a passage of time that so much of the experience of the place seems to deny. "There had been no years," he says, and "it was all the same." He virtually chants:

> Summertime, oh, summertime, pattern of life indelible, the fade proof lake, the woods unshatterable, the pasture with the sweetfern and the juniper forever and ever, summer without end; this was the background,

(Belgrade Lakes, Maine) 33

and the life along the shore was the design, the cottages with their in-
nocent and tranquil design, their tiny docks with the flagpole and the
American flag floating against the white clouds in the blue sky, the little
paths over the roots of the trees leading from camp to camp and the path
leading back to the outhouses and the can of lime for sprinkling, and at
the souvenir counters at the store the miniature birch-bark canoes and
the post cards that showed things looking a little better than they looked.

Toward the end of the essay White gives an overview of what their
week was like: "The bass were biting well and the sun shone endlessly, day after day. We would be tired at night and lie down in the
accumulated heat of the little bedrooms after the long hot day and
the breeze would stir almost imperceptibly outside and the smell of
the swamp drift in through the rusty screens." All of this stirs his
memory with Proustian clarity and detail—"I kept remembering everything, lying in bed in the morning"—and as they continue doing
things together and this long paragraph is filled with the first person plural ("We would go up to the store. . . . We would walk out. . . .
We explored the streams . . . we lay on the town wharf"), he declares:
"Everywhere we went I had trouble making out which was I, the one
walking at my side, the one walking in my pants."

Then there is a long paragraph with a single *I* in it ("like the re-
vival of an old melodrama that I had seen long ago") describing a kind
of universal summer thunderstorm. "The second-act climax of the
drama of the electrical disturbance over a lake in America had not
changed in any important respect. This was the big scene, still the
big scene." He describes the storm: "The whole thing was so familiar, the first feeling of oppression and heat and a general air around
camp of not wanting to go very far away. In midafternoon (it was all
the same) a curious darkening of the sky, and a lull in everything that
had made life tick." It's as if the narrator draws back from his own
experience by leaving out verbs and actors until the storm begins to
abate, and even then he refers to the campers generally, "running
out in joy and relief to go swimming in the rain, their bright cries

The Pattern of Life Indelible

perpetuating the deathless joke about how they were getting simply drenched, and the children screaming with delight at the new sensation of bathing in the rain, and the joke about getting drenched linking the generations in a strong indestructible chain. And the comedian who waded in carrying an umbrella."

But then he tells us that his son decides to join the swimmers and takes down his rain-soaked trunks from the clothesline. "Languidly, and with no thought of going in, I watched him, his hard little body, skinny and bare, saw him wince slightly as he pulled up around his vitals the small, soggy, icy garment. As he buckled the swollen belt, suddenly my groin felt the chill of death."

I don't know how many times now I have read and reread the essay, but the way it leads us gullibly, serenely toward the conclusion always affects me, always makes me feel a jolt at the concluding paragraph, always make me look back at all those instances where there was foreshadowing or foreboding—"perpetuating the deathless joke," for instance, or the generations linked "in a strong, indestructible chain." This is essay as lyric, as elegy on a theme of mutability, both as plainspoken and as poetic as the "language men do use" in a Wordsworthian ode. When we consider the music of its language, its rhythms and repetitions, and the way it is as cunningly crafted as a Hemingway short story, both in language and in emotion, it's easy to agree with the essayist Joseph Epstein that "Once More to the Lake" is "dazzling and devastating, art of a heightened kind that an essayist is rarely privileged to achieve."

iii. The Rain in Maine 2002

Because Bear Springs Camp had been booked all month, we were staying in a bed and breakfast inn in the village of Belgrade Lakes, located on a narrow strip of land between Great Pond to the east and Long Pond to the west. When I drove back from the camp on the North Bay of Great Pond, I found my wife working on research on the screened-in backward-L-shaped porch on the western front on the inn. We put our notebooks away and changed our clothes to go canoeing, and as we stepped outside, the thunder that had been booming faintly in the east grew louder, and the sky darkened. On the front doorstep of the inn, just as we changed the plan to a walk down to a tavern, the wind picked up, and the innkeeper, who had just begun to mow the lawn, wheeled the riding mower around and headed back to the barn, and the wind gusted strongly, and we went back inside and settled back on the porch. Within minutes the storm was upon us, the peals of thunder regular and almost deafening, the lightning less noticeable through all the trees except when it flashed close enough that, the boom following immediately, we were sure it had struck down by the water.

The wind grew less persistent and gusty, but the rain came thick and hard. We sat on the screened-in porch and listened to it churn and hiss and splatter, watched it drop on two sides of us as if we were sitting behind an L-shaped waterfall. The thunder rumbled deep after every boom, rolled off into the distance. The south side of the house had a narrow strip of garden and a little way beyond it a wall of tall thick maples shielding the house from the town, so we couldn't see very deeply into the storm. On the west side the usual view of an open lawn and a scattering of older, larger trees, lawn furniture, a wishing well, a stand of wood lilies, was nearly invisible behind the translucent rain-beaded screen.

As White had written, "This was the big scene, still the big scene," and the thunder seemed to be playing the score for percussion as he had described it: "The premonitory rumble. Then the kettle drum, then the snare, then the bass drum and cymbals." Listening to the whole orchestration of storm, I wondered about the people at Bear Springs Camp, imagined them huddled in their cabins, the rain heavier and closer on their metal roofs, lake and sky merging in one liquid flow, the air thick with the windows closed but cooling where the screen door protected by the porch roof would be open.

The storm rumbled persistently as it passed, and then the rain lessened, and the sky to the west brightened, and the beads in the front screen began to disintegrate of their own weight so that the view

The Pattern of Life Indelible

cleared somewhat. Unseen traffic on the road in front of the yard now sometimes drowned out the sounds of the storm. Birdcalls came again and with the brightening sky the return of shadows. And then, while the trees and the roofs continued to drip, the storm was over.

Later, after dinner, sitting out on the porch, we noticed the gleaming sky. It was sunset, but the glow was so bright that we strolled down to Peninsula Park across the street for a clear, unobstructed view across Long Pond of the spectacular sky. The pond was a deep blue tending toward black, the hills along the distant shore were black, but behind the hills the sky was on fire, dazzlingly golden, gleaming yellow-orange and tinting the clouds pink and red. To the north some clouds shaped like mountain ranges hung in dark blue against the blue-gray of the night sky, and between them and us lower translucent clouds hung like ponds at the base of hills. We could see the dark clouds through the transparent clouds, and they seemed to be casting their shadows on water, like the real hills and real shadows and real water below. At times the mountain range clouds would rise enough so that they seemed a distant range with a bank of fog filling the intervening valley. Then a cool breeze picked up, and as the sun, invisible in the west, sank lower, it pulled the golden sky after it like a curtain.

iv. Once More to the Lake 1941

When I look at "Once More to the Lake" as an essay of place—as, that is, an essay in which the evocation of setting is central to the development of theme or character or action—I am aware of how much it is suffused by the author's familiarity with the landscape and the routine behaviors of the people who have populated it over time. White is a significantly elegiac essayist, the darkness or brooding undercurrent that many of his critics have noted in his amiable pose as a temperate observer of the everyday often growing out of his awareness of time passing and his distrust of headlong, intemperate change. Not only his frequent returns to Great Pond but also his long residency near a small, out-of-the-way Maine village attest to his preference for a relatively simple, relatively repetitive lifestyle (a word I'm sure he would never willingly use). One of the hallmarks of the nonfiction of place is its success in evoking in the reader familiar with the setting a recognition, sometimes uncomfortable, of the accuracy and insight of the recreation—it may be inevitable that some readers will disagree with the essayist's interpretation of life in that setting, but they will still be able to say, "Yes, I know this place; this account is true to the place where I live." A second, connected hallmark of the nonfiction of place is its ability to trigger in the reader *unfamiliar* with the setting a similar sense of having been there, to provoke the ability to dwell within the textual place. This is, after all, what armchair travelers are seeking to achieve, a sense of having lived in a space they have never inhabited except vicariously. I would argue that, in the most successful nonfiction of place, both kinds of readers, insiders and outsiders, feel they are in the same space, feel they would know the space again if they visited it.

The intimacy that the writer evidences with the place in the essay arises from long familiarity with it. According to his biographer, White came with his family to Belgrade Lakes for the first time in August 1905 (not 1904), and the annual monthly stay at a camp on Great Pond continued for several years. In 1914 White took a friend, Frederick Schuler, to Snug Harbor Camps and wrote and illustrated a pamphlet for Freddie describing the place. As an adult, he returned to Great Pond and stayed at Bert Mosher's Bear Springs Camp on his own—for example, he abruptly disappeared from his job at the *New Yorker* in September of 1927 and wrote his editor from Belgrade, and in January 1929 he stayed with Bert Mosher and ice-skated on Great Pond. In 1936, shortly after his mother died in May and nearly a year after his father's death in August 1935, he wrote to his brother Stanley from Bert Mosher's camp. Stanley was eight years older and had been White's most important playmate during the early days in Maine. The letter to Stanley suggests that White's association of Belgrade Lakes with changelessness was connected with intimate and inevitable issues of mortality raised by the loss of their parents but

The Pattern of Life Indelible

that White, who to that point had never written essays expressly about his personal life, wasn't ready to deal with these issues in a public piece of writing. Yet the letter to Stanley establishes a pattern of thematic repetition that would surface later in "Once More to the Lake."

He started the letter: "I returned to Belgrade. Things haven't changed much." On the Bar Harbor Express, "when you look out of the window in the diner, steam is rising from the pastures and the sun is out, and pretty soon the train is skirting a blue lake called Messalonski. Things don't change much." The letter continues a litany of description in present tense: "The lake hangs clear and still at dawn. . . . In the shallows along shore the pebbles and driftwood show clear and smooth on bottom, and black water bugs dart, spreading a wake and a shadow. . . . The water in the basin is icy before breakfast, and cuts sharply into your nose and ears and makes your face blue as you wash. . . . The insides of your camp are hung with pictures cut from magazines, and the camp smells of lumber and damp. Things don't change much." The letter is one long paragraph of description, recounting in detail the continuous present. "You buy a drink of Birch Beer at Bean's tackle store. Big bass swim lazily in the deep water at the end of the wharf, well fed. Long lean guide boats kick white water in the stern until they suck under. There are still one cylinder engines that don't go. Maybe it's the needle valve." He concludes: "Yes, sir, I returned to Belgrade, and things don't change much. I thought somebody ought to know."

By the time White went once more to the lake with his son, Joel, in July 1941, he was writing a monthly column for *Harper's Magazine* called "One Man's Meat" that required him regularly to fill a designated space in the magazine. On July 24 he wrote his wife, Katharine, that "Joe has been in [the lake] for more than an hour without showing the slightest tendency to come out. He is a devotee of fresh water swimming at the moment, and it really does seem good to have warm bathing for a change." He explained what they had been doing and how they had "a perfectly enormous outboard motor on our rowboat," which he had difficulty starting and which lurched up to speed with jarring power. "I miss the old one-cylinder gas engine of yesteryear which made a fine peaceful sound across the water. This is too much like living on the edge of an airfield." But nonetheless he was enthusiastic about being there. "This place is as American as a drink of Coca Cola. The white collar family having its annual liberty. I must say it seems sort of good. . . . Everybody you've ever seen on Main Street or on Elm Avenue is here."

These two letters foreshadow much of the language and many of the subthemes of "Once More to the Lake." In the opening paragraphs, for example, he mentions the "fearful cold of the sea-water" making him long for "the placidity of a lake in the woods" and how his son "had never had any fresh water up his nose." His mantra from the letter to Stanley changes only slightly ("there had been no years"; "it was all the same"), and his descriptions echo earlier ones: "In the shallows, the dark, watersoaked sticks and twigs, smooth and old, were undulating in clusters on the bottom against the clean ribbed sand, and the track of the mussel was plain." Or: "My boy loved our rented outboard, and his great desire was to achieve singlehanded mastery over it, and authority, and he soon learned the trick of choking it a little (but not too much), and the adjustment of the needle valve." The language is more deliberately chosen and its rhythms more carefully modulated—White claimed to write by ear and his manuscripts show the effort to revise for sound and pace—but again and again the earlier letters echo in the essay.

Whether White consulted the letters again before writing the essay or not—as any journal keeper knows, transcribing your thoughts often locks them in your memory in retrievable form—one of the distinguishing qualities of this essay is its long gestation period. White was forty-two when he wrote it (it was submitted to the magazine for its August 1941 deadline and published untitled in the "One Man's Meat" department that October), and he had been observing Great Pond and rehearsing his reflections upon it for at least thirty-six years. Perhaps, in addition to its affecting power, what contributes greatly to the sense of place that underlies the essay is its aura of lived experience, its simultaneous superimposition of place and persona on the page. In the nonfiction of place the author's persona is not simply situated in place; more compellingly, place is situated within—and emerges from—the author.

v. Great Pond 2002

On our final morning at Belgrade Lakes I went out to visit the camp one last time. In the interval between my first visit and my last, I had taken in the terrain from a couple of different levels. I had climbed a few local mountains in search of an overview of the landscape and seen northwoods forest sweeping away in every direction, open to the sky only where the ponds were. I knew this impression of vast wilderness was illusory; White himself says of Great Pond, "The lake had not been what you would call a wild lake. There were cottages sprinkled around the shores, and it was in farming country, although the shores of the lake were heavily wooded." I knew that the camp itself had been constructed on a farm, and, as with so many camps of this kind, the farmhouse served as the office and communal dining hall and operations center. For much of the early part of the twentieth century, when there were many camps on the Maine lakes, the camps were a way for the farmers to diversify and subsidize their farming. Now most of the camps were gone, and Bear Springs Camp was one of the few still operating pretty much as it had in the past, improvements in plumbing and accessibility and leisure toy construction being the principle variables. Across Maine, across New England, in the decline of farming, in the wake of emigration westward, the forests had returned and now feigned permanence, immutability. When we left Belgrade Lakes, we would drive only twenty miles or so to Vienna (pronounced "vye-enna"), to watch friends celebrate the village's bicentennial and to walk the woods of their lot, much of which had been field, pasture, and woodlot two hundred years ago.

We had also seen Great Pond from lake level. We rented a canoe from an outfitter on the quiet waterway that cuts through the village of Belgrade Lakes and connects Long Pond to Great Pond and paddled out onto Great Pond. The lake itself was moderately choppy and windswept, and we had to paddle continuously to gain ground, staying near the shore, running out into the lake only to avoid docks and rafts and anchored boats and empty anchors and, occasionally, shoals. It was surprisingly quiet much of the time—occasionally, someone would speed through the center of the lake, and we would contend with mild wakes, or a pontoon boat would charge away from the dock in front of someone's house, but most of the time we saw nobody but an older woman reading a novel on her dock, a few elderly people sitting on lounge chairs under an umbrella, and, toward the end of our outing, four youngsters in kayaks venturing out from their cottage while someone's father stopped reading on the dock long enough to tie up the dogs that kept jumping in the water trying to follow the kids.

It had been good to see the shoreline from the lake, though we didn't go around to Bear Springs Camp but only tested the waters. These were mostly private homes, perhaps a few inns or B&B's or rentals, no camps, but the well-to-do who could afford these places seemed to me to not be moved by much different desires than the people at Bear Springs Camp—the desire to relax, to get away, to luxuriate in downtime. The upscale private cottages were no doubt further upscale than they had been sixty years earlier, but the "American family taking its annual liberty" on Great Pond seemed to have largely maintained the same demographics as in White's experience.

To wind things up, I felt I needed to circumnavigate Great Pond by car, so I drove south first, then rounded the southern end and followed the road up the east side in search of Horse Point Road and a view of North Bay. At a Boy Scout camp at the end of the road I gazed through binoculars at Bear Springs Camp across the bay, idling in the sun, the woods rising behind it. It seemed a small narrow strip between the wide strips of blue sky, green forest, blue lake, completely insignificant from the opposite shoreline and probably content to be inconspicuous, unlike some of the private homes farther out on Jamaica Point. When I stopped at a higher point along the road, over-

The Pattern of Life Indelible

looking a busy quarry digging away the side of the hill, I couldn't see the camp at all.

I circled back around to the camp then, parked on the road in the same shady spot I had before, and walked down the dirt road to the central beach. It was a cooler day, and the beach was less active than it had been, though I was there around the same time of day. Boys were hitting golf ball– and softball-sized Wiffle Balls, and a woman in a swimsuit was taking pictures of her family in front of their cabin, but no one was in the water except for a middle-aged man who took out a kayak as I arrived and, in the distance, a single fisherman and one lone Jet Skier. In front of the beachfront cabins there were a few idlers, but not much was going on.

The sky was a perfect blue with perfectly wispy clouds to break up that unblemished blue. The wind was very light and the water the same blue as the sky, the same placid attitude. From the end of the dock I took pictures of North Bay, of the shoreline, of the gigantic spruce that must be the oldest tree on the farm, of the creek winding through the sand to empty on the beach. Then I took my time walking back up the road toward the office–farmhouse–dining hall. Two teenage girls were taking turns with the payphone at the end of the porch, one of them someone I had seen earlier near the cabins, talking on a cell phone. Peg Churchill and her mother and two daughters were in the office, not doing much. Peg was pleasant, polite, but reserved. I told her who I was and why I was there, and she seemed content to show no reaction or interest. In order to seem to have more purpose in my presence, I asked if I could see a photo of E. B. White that I had read about in an article about the place, and she went in the family room to get it.

The picture is a five-by-seven-inch blowup from a snapshot and shows White, perhaps in his eighties or late seventies at the youngest, pulling away from shore in his canoe. He is thin but barrel-chested, his plaid short-sleeved shirt unbuttoned, exposing his white chest and stomach, his tan or beige shorts almost matching his white legs. He is sockless, wearing sneakers or deck shoes, and he has a billed cap on his head and sunglasses. He seems energetic, if not strong, and concentrates on paddling the canoe. One of the cabins and a dock and a stretch of shoreline make up the background of the picture. He could be any other camper, simply engaged in a commonplace leisure activity.

I thanked her for the look at the picture, tried vainly to lure her into small talk, failed, and departed. Outside I ran into the woman from New Jersey coming from the guest laundry. She asked if I had any luck getting a reservation, then told me as we parted that she and her family would be here another week before they went back. As I walked back to my car, I thought, perhaps zanily, that I at least knew something of what it was to spend time here, connect to people, and depart. In spite of the interval of time and the circumstances of my presence here, I had been to E. B. White's Great Pond. (It was all the same.) Thanks to his essay, and the refusal of the place itself to change very much, I, who had never been here before, had come once more to the lake.

*

The Pattern of Life Indelible

The Everlastingly Great Look of the Sky
(Walden Pond, Massachusetts)

Then to Walden pond, that beautifully embower'd sheet of water, and spent over an hour there. On the spot in the woods where Thoreau had his solitary house is now quite a cairn of stones, to mark the place; I too carried one and deposited on the heap.

—WALT WHITMAN, *Specimen Days*

Walden 2002

Miss Nims, take a letter to E. B. White. Dear Andy: I thought of you the other day as I was approaching Concord on Route 2A. That is, I was on Route 2A, approaching Concord, in July 2002, and thought of you when you were on Route 62, approaching Concord, in June 1939, which you describe at the start of the epistolary essay you wrote about your visit there. You published the essay first in your monthly column for *Harper's*, "One Man's Meat," then reprinted it under the title "Walden" when you collected your best columns in *One Man's Meat*. That essay is one of my favorites in the book, and the book is one of my favorites of all time, a book I've reread about as often as I've reread *Walden* by Henry Thoreau. That's one of the reasons I like the essay, of course, because we both share an enthusiasm for *Walden*, which you described as "a document of increasing pertinence" and the "best written and the cockiest . . . tale of individual simplicity." Like you, I think *Walden* is a very wise and humorous book, and many of Thoreau's sentences have stuck in my memory—and surfaced in my syntax—as much as they have in yours or (to be honest) as much as yours have in mine.

I may as well admit that, as you had, I was journeying to Concord with the deliberate intention of visiting Thoreau's wood but also that I had already spent a week in Maine at, as you once put it, "places where [your] spoor may still be found." Not only did I visit Great Pond, the lake of "Once More to the Lake," but I took a day to drive to and from Brooklin, where you lived in a colonial farmhouse and where you and your wife and your son are buried. You claimed "never to have knelt at the grave of a philosopher nor placed wreaths on moldy poets," but you placed a stone on the cairn by Thoreau's cabin, as I intended to do. I would have placed a stone on your grave as well, but I knew you'd disapprove, and I didn't want to set a bad example for others. Walden Pond was the only pilgrimage you felt obliged to make; I have a few more idols than you, but after Walden and Maine, I only need to visit Montaigne's tower to complete my pilgrimages.

As you pointed out about your own motives, my purpose in going to Walden Pond, like Henry's, was not to live cheaply or to live dearly there but to transact some private business with the fewest obstacles. Like you, I expected to write about my visit, but I also expected to write about your visit as well, though that hadn't always been my intention. I'd originally thought only of comparing your description of Great Pond with Henry's description of Walden Pond, and that's what I'd set out to accomplish, until I remembered your Walden essay while I was wandering in Brooklin and photocopied it out of a volume you'd signed and given to the Friend Memorial Library.

I suspected it was the right thing to do when I ran into Mary Lush in the cemetery. As she had since girlhood many years before, she returned to Brooklin each year to visit family and friends, some now in the cemetery. We met because she wanted to show me the grave of Smoky Joe, Gentleman Cat, owner unidentified, but she'd seen me by the White family plot and told me that, years earlier, she'd met you once when you'd come to her cousin's for some fresh crabmeat and stayed to chat with some of the family. It turned out she was a docent at the museum in Concord, where I was heading next, and I promised to talk to her about Thoreau then. A funny bit of synchronicity there, running into one author's docent at the grave of another author she'd also known. So, I could hardly help thinking of E. B. White as I drove into Concord intending to think about Thoreau.

I arrived in Concord around midmorning, and at the Concord Museum I did speak to Mary Lush, if only for a few minutes. Two exhibits in the museum especially attracted me. One was Emerson's study, transferred from his nearby house for preservation; it is generally underlit and gray but filled with books and an atmosphere of intellectual activity. The other was the Thoreau gallery, which displayed the writing desk, chair, and cot he had used in his cabin at the pond. It reminded me of Jill Krementz's well-known photograph of you at your writing table, Andy, the one you captioned for your wife: "This is a writer trying to look like a writer when he knows full well he is being photographed." You wrote in a boathouse, not a cabin. You said once, in "A Slight Sound at Evening," written for the *Walden* centennial, "Thoreau might find it instructive that this memorial essay is being written in a house that, through no intent on my part, is the same size and shape as his own domicile on the pond—about ten by fifteen, tight, plainly finished, and at a little distance from my Concord." You added, "Here in the boathouse I am a wilder and, it would appear, a healthier man, by a safe margin. I have a chair, a bench, a table, and I can walk into the water if I tire of the land." Your house too fronted a cove. (I had to look that quote up—what I remembered at the moment of standing before the cabin display was the black-and-white image of your boathouse, as Spartan and as spare and as serviceable as Thoreau's cabin.) The association of the two dwellings made me feel more comfortable in Concord.

In the heat of the afternoon I walked out to Sleepy Hollow Cemetery to visit Authors' Ridge, where Thoreau and Emerson are buried. The tourist traffic around the graves was lively—most people simply drove to the base of the ridge rather than trudge through the village and the cemetery to reach it—but in moments when I felt driven away from Henry's grave, I jotted in my daybook and reflected on others who had been there. Walt Whitman, visiting Concord in September

1881, was taken to Nathaniel Hawthorne's and Thoreau's graves— Thoreau's, he said, "had a brown headstone, moderately elaborate, with inscriptions"—and later spent an hour at Walden Pond, where he placed a stone on the cairn commemorating Thoreau; eight months later he returned to stand by the grave of Emerson, who had died in April 1882. John Muir, who had known Emerson but not Thoreau, made the trip in 1893 and left flowers on the graves of both Thoreau and Emerson. On my visit, too, I saw flowers, both fresh and wilted, as well as stones on Henry's grave.

I finished my first day in Concord much as you had, Andy. I had dinner at the inn and strolled around town. It was early August, and the evening was hot and muggy, and the town was bustling with tourists and summer visitors. Traffic was heavy and parking sparse, and people seemed to sag from the heat and the long hours of walking through historic houses and battlegrounds and shops. I spent a quiet hour in a good bookshop, buying an edition of Hawthorne's essay on the Old Manse to read in bed that night and a book about the Concord landscape in Thoreau's time to help me understand the same landscape in mine.

Walden 1939

Throughout his writing life E. B. White often made reference to Thoreau and was once described by James Thurber as carrying a pocket-sized copy of *Walden* with him wherever he went. "A Slight Sound at Evening," originally published as "Walden 1954" in the *Yale Review* and subsequently as an introduction to an edition of *Walden*, is one of White's few sustained articles of literary criticism. The essay "Walden," from *One Man's Meat*, is more typical of him. It begins: "Miss Nims, take a letter to Henry Thoreau. Dear Henry: I thought of you the other day . . ." and largely maintains the epistolary tone throughout as the author recounts his experiences in Concord. Much of his focus is on lightly comparing Thoreau's time with his own.

White, for instance, claims that what made him think of Thoreau was the way a woman mowing a lawn seemed to be struggling to keep up with her power mower. He observes, "Concord hasn't changed much, Henry; the farm implements and the animals still have the upper hand." Later, describing "the stupefaction a day's motor journey induces," he writes, "It was a delicious evening, Henry, where the whole body is one sense and imbibes delight through every pore, if I may coin a phrase. Fields were richly brown where the harrow, drawn by the stripped Ford, had lately sunk its teeth; pastures were green; and overhead the sky had that same everlasting great look that you will find on page 144 of the Oxford pocket edition." (It's page 161 of the standard Princeton edition.) Often echoing or adapting Thoreau's language, White explores changes in the town and the society over the course of nearly a century, generally finding an enduring pertinence to Thoreau's observations. Boys building a hut in a vacant lot suggest to him that "they too were escaping from town, to live naturally, in a rich blend of savagery and philosophy." He compares the sound of the Fitchburg train that Thoreau had described with the sound of cars on Concord streets: "Automobiles, skirting a village green, are like flies that have gained the inner ear—they buzz, cease, pause, start, shift, stop, halt, brake, and the whole effect is a nervous polytone curiously disturbing." He explains his reference to the radio show *Amos and Andy* with one Thoreauvian phrase ("it is a drama of many scenes and without an end") and the modern need to number highways with another ("Men have an indistinct notion that if they keep up this activity long enough all will at length ride somewhere, in next to no time").

When White walks out to Walden Pond on the morning of his second day in Concord, he suggests that the Golden Pheasant lunchroom, near the pond, should sell "rice, Indian meal, and molasses—just for old time's sake" along with the Sealtest ice cream and frankfurters it advertises. He designates the inhabitants of Walden Breezes, a trailer park, as Thoreau's "philosophical descendants [dwelling] in their trailers, each trailer the size of your hut. . . . Trailer people leave the city, as you did, to discover solitude and in any weather, at any hour day or night, to improve the nick of time; but they soon collect in villages and get bogged deeper in the mud than ever."

Throughout the essay White balances his tone between irony and elegy, an awareness of how comically banal contemporary life seems compared to Thoreau's transcendental idealism and at the same time an acceptance of his own complicity in that banality. At the pond he is torn between surprised reverence and wry disappointment, the contrast most apparent in his feeling "strangely excited suddenly to be snooping around your premises, tiptoeing along watchfully, as though not to tread by mistake upon the intervening century." He walks toward the site of the cabin and experiences both a sense of connection with the past and an abrupt connection with the present: "I heard your frog, a full, clear *troonk*, guiding me, still hoarse and solemn, bridging the years. . . . But he soon quit, and I came on a couple of young boys throwing stones at him."

To this point in the essay the sense of place White has given us has chiefly been suburban or small town filtered through the prism of Thoreauvian reference. Without those echoes from *Walden*, the reader would not connect the town White visits with the community Thoreau wrote about. The most descriptive passage in this essay, the one that most solidly grounds us in the landscape, comes when White arrives at the site of Thoreau's cabin:

> Your front yard is marked by a bronze tablet set in a stone. Four small granite posts, a few feet away, show where the house was. On top of the tablet was a pair of faded blue bathing trunks with a white stripe. Back of it is a pile of stones, a sort of cairn, left by your visitors as a tribute I suppose. It is a rather ugly little heap of stones, Henry. In fact the hillside itself seems faded, browbeaten; a few tall skinny pines, bare of lower limbs, a smattering of young maples in suitable green, some birches and oaks, and a number of trees felled by the last big wind. It was from the bole of one of these fallen pines, torn up by the roots, that I extracted the stone that I added to the cairn—a sentimental act in which I was in-

The Everlastingly Great Look of the Sky

terrupted by a small terrier from a nearby picnic group, who confronted me and wanted to know about the stone.

I sat down for a while on one of the posts of your house to listen to the bluebottles and the dragonflies. The invaded glade sprawled shabby and mean at my feet, but the flies were tuned to the old vibration. There were the remains of a fire in your ruins, but I doubt that it was yours; also two beer bottles trodden into the soil and become part of earth. A young oak had taken root in your house, and two or three ferns, unrolling like the ticklers at a banquet. The only other furnishings were a DuBarry pattern sheet, a page torn from a picture magazine, and some crusts in wax paper.

The emphasis in the description falls on the changes that have taken place in the glade and the way the litter of the present intrudes upon the tranquillity of the past.

The essay is not so much an homage to *Walden* (as "A Slight Sound at Evening" may be considered, with its efforts to explain the enduring pertinence of the book) as a wry and somewhat self-deprecating commentary on the ways the world surrounding Walden Pond has, inevitably perhaps, failed to measure up to the standard Thoreau set. White includes himself in this mild indictment. In the conclusion of the essay he reports on his expenses in a manner similar to the itemized list Thoreau provided in the "Economy" chapter and points out that his expenses for a day are almost what Thoreau spent for eight months. The items include a baseball bat and fielder's glove for his son, "the kind of impediment with which you were never on even terms. . . . You never had to cope with a shortstop."

White often used an ending that turned back on the author, making light of his ego or his shortcomings, and here the admission highlights White's distance as a husband, father, and average citizen from Thoreau's self-conscious and earnest idealism. At the same time, it may suggest Thoreau's shortcomings, as someone who was able to be an idealist because he was unencumbered by the kind of commitments the rest of society lives with every day. In "A Slight Sound at Evening," written fifteen years after "Walden," White acknowledged the unspecified conflict of his earlier essay when he observed, "A little band of dedicated Thoreauvians would be a sorry sight indeed: fellows who hate compromise and have compromised, fellows who love wildness and have lived tamely, and at their side, censuring them and chiding them, the ghostly figure of this upright man. . . . I should hate to be called a Thoreauvian, yet I wince every time I walk into the barn I'm pushing before me, seventy-five feet by forty, and the author of *Walden* has served as my conscience through the long stretches of my trivial days" (241).

Walden 2002

It's early yet on Walden Pond. Two boats with tiny motors and a canoe traverse the waters in the distance. Along the shady beach a few earnest swimmers have been working through the water, some with goggles, one with a rubber suit to guard against chill. The pond is popular with distance swimmers. Other people, less streamlined, sit idly in the shade on their own beach chairs, and on an unpopulated section of beach two children fish under their grandmother's supervision. Not far off I hear the drone of a plane circling the area and the hum and whoosh of traffic on Route 126, the road I drove to get here. New arrivals, draped in towels, beach bags, and folding canvas chairs, come strolling down the path from the parking lots— the pond has a one thousand–person capacity limit, and by 8:30 we are only up to thirty or so. I too am tempted by the water, gleaming blue at the center of the pond, glassy green closer to shore, all riffled lightly by a pleasant cool breeze, but I decide to wait until the oppressive heat of yesterday returns.

Somewhat self-consciously, I saunter off through the woods to the site of Thoreau's cabin, some distance from the main beach area. To the west of Walden Pond I hear the sound of the railroad, as Thoreau heard it on the Fitchburg Line. It trails off in the distance, and sounds of nature—the squawk of a blue jay, the whistle of a chickadee, the cackles and warbles of other birds I can't identify, cicadas

The Everlastingly Great Look of the Sky

just starting up nearby, a symphony or at least a chamber ensemble of instruments with occasional percussion from squirrels and chipmunks—take its place, train call now diminuendo by distance. Traffic thrum and muted jet roar sometimes interrupt, but otherwise this is the sound of Walden Pond as Thoreau heard it.

It's been over twenty years since I was last at the site of the cabin. The cairn of stones has ballooned into almost talus proportions; the stone markers for the dimensions of the house and the woodshed are still simple, even austere. The "overgrown slope" where Thoreau and friends constructed the cabin is plentifully reforested, and the new trails around the woods include a scenic path through young white pines that Henry would have never seen. Bathers float in Thoreau Cove, and hikers cross Wyman Meadow to get to the cove from the road. The woods are crisscrossed with trails that are both deliberate and inadvertent, but as I quietly sit here, only one elderly swimmer passes on a nearby trail, bound for a spot on the shore farthest from the beach. Walden Pond's shoreline is really all beach now.

For two years, two months, and two days, Henry Thoreau lived deliberately here, on Emerson's woodlot by Walden Pond, before he decided he had "several more lives to live" and moved back into town, to continue writing *Walden* and keep his journal and be a saunterer in Concord. I think it good that the site is here and reverenced and that the crusade against condominiums and development has succeeded. But I notice that I am the only pilgrim to the site this morning; the rest of the pilgrims make their journey to the pond and the sun, like the young woman who just went down another path carrying a beach chair and a backpack, never glancing up the trail to the cabin site.

From where she and, earlier, the old man passed, you can see the sign in front of the cairn on which is engraved these words: "I went to the woods because I wished to live deliberately, to front only the essential facts of life, and see if I could not learn what it had to teach, and not, when I came to die, discover that I had not lived at all." This is a different purpose than those have who swim and sun and fish and lollygag along the shore today. It would be difficult to distinguish

Walden Pond from the shores on any other summer lake except that the motorboats do not sound and the Jet Skis are not allowed.

As I sit journaling on a tree stump off to one side of the site, two more sightseers amble down the trail, she in brown pants and red tank top, he in shorts, flowered shirt, and cap. He is carrying a videotape camcorder and leads her back up the trail a ways in order to stage a scene in which he walks down and points at the center of the cabin. Now he records the explanatory billboard in front of the site and shoots a close-up of the engraving on one of the posts, oblivious to a fire siren in the distance creating his soundtrack. He circles the site, choosing his shots and letting the camera run long enough that they will be able to read the signs when they play the tape at home. His companion points out the quote in front of the cabin; he reads it slowly, records it deliberately, thoroughly, then pans the setting. They fuss to put away the camcorder, and she takes out a cheap disposable FunPak camera.

She takes pictures of him standing by the quote sign and squatting by the cairn, then comes around for a still of the site sign—I scribble on, trying to seem absorbed in my work, while he directs her shot of him hunkering by the sign with the cabin posts behind him. Then they walk away, taking with them considerable evidence of his presence at the site. I wonder what it means to him to have been here.

It is also fair to ask what it means to me to have been here, who come as both pilgrim and acolyte (of sorts) as well as tourist and scholar. I am drawn here by Thoreau's sense of place and the power with which he conveyed it 150 years ago, but I can't kid myself that this is the same physical place or that it meant to others in his own time what it meant to him, what it means to us when we read his book, what it means to us at a distance. I gaze up at the towering oaks, maples, white pines—trees Thoreau would have never seen—and set off to complete my circuit of the pond.

By now it's nearly noon, and the heat and humidity have risen with the sun. I find bathers all along the shore, and the public beach area is thronging with people. The paths I follow above the shore are en-

The Everlastingly Great Look of the Sky

closed with rusted metal poles and black plastic-coated wire fencing to keep the public from harming the shoreline—part of a restoration scheme that weathers the path thoroughly. At frequent breaks in the fencing a few stone steps lead to the shoreline, mitigating the effects of access, and the inland side of the path is lined with boulders holding back erosion. On the south shore I go down to the beach and trudge along the water's edge, follow it back around to the beach house and the road.

Near the parking lot across the road from the pond I drift by the replica of Thoreau's cabin that workmen are still completing. It smells of fresh sawdust. It's built to specifications gleaned from Thoreau's records and from the archaeological evidence—the hut itself is utterly gone, but the site was excavated to uncover its foundations—and furnished with replicas of the three chairs, cot, writing desk, and cast iron stove on display at the Concord Museum. A statue of Thoreau in an odd, awkward posture stands in front of it. A steady stream of swimmers shuffles past the cabin from the crowded parking lot, only a handful stopping to read the large sign near it or to step inside. The cabin may serve as a reminder of Thoreau's presence at the pond, but it also serves to emphasize how little the place resembles the pond he knew.

Walden 1845–1847

Walden is permeated by Thoreau's sense of place. His two years in the cabin, from 1845 to 1847, were not the limit of his experience at the pond, which he had known since childhood and would continue to visit in the years he spent writing the book, finally published in 1854, right through to his death in 1862. The Thoreau gallery of the Concord Museum has posted on the wall this observation from his journal (January 1, 1858): "I have lately been surveying the Walden woods so extensively and minutely that now I see it mapped on my mind's eye,—as, indeed, on paper,—as so many men's wood-lots, and am aware that when I walk there I am at a given moment passing from such a one's wood-lot to another's. I fear this particular dry knowledge may affect my imagination and fancy, that it will not be easy to see so much wildness and native vigor there as formerly."

He'd left his cabin more than ten years earlier, and he worried about his perspective on the woods changing, but he also knew that it had been a woodlot when he built his cabin in the first place. He was, after all, building on Emerson's woodlot, like any woodlot a fuel resource for stove and fireplace. This was second-growth forest in a populous countryside, and in Thoreau's time New England was as developed an agrarian society as it would ever be. Only after the Civil War, when industrialization and westward immigration invited abandonment of farm communities, did the hayfields and croplands revert to woodland again. In Thoreau's time it was a considerably open countryside.

Thoreau's description of Walden Pond begins when he locates his cabin in the second chapter of *Walden*, "Where I Lived and What I Lived For": "I was seated by the shore of a small pond, about a mile and a half south of the village of Concord and somewhat higher than it, in the midst of an extensive wood between that town and Lincoln, and about two miles south of that our only field known to fame, Concord Battle Ground; but I was so low in the woods that the opposite shore, half a mile off, like the rest, covered with wood, was my most distant horizon." He soon provides a view of the pond from a different perspective: "From a hill top near by, where the wood had been recently cut off, there was a pleasing vista southward across the pond, through a wide indentation in the hills which form the shore there," which gave him a view "between and over the near green hills to some distant and higher ones in the horizon, tinged with blue." Beyond them he could see, on tiptoe, "a glimpse of some of the peaks of the still bluer and more distant mountain ranges in the north-west . . . and also of some portion of the village." But this really only gives the larger setting and the sense of his boundaries.

In later chapters Thoreau is more specific about place. The "Solitude" chapter opens with a vivid account of an evening walk:

This is a delicious evening, when the whole body is one sense, and imbibes delight through every pore. I go and come with a strange liberty in Nature, a part of herself. As I walk along the stony shore of the pond in my shirt sleeves, though it is cool as well as cloudy and windy, and I see nothing special to attract me, all the elements are unusually congenial to me. The bullfrogs trump to usher in the night, and the note of the whippoorwill is borne on the rippling wind from over the water. Sympathy with the fluttering alder and poplar leaves almost takes away my breath; yet, like the lake, my serenity is rippled but not ruffled. These small waves raised by the evening wind are as remote from storm as the smooth reflecting surface. Though it is now dark, the wind still blows and roars in the wood, the waves still dash, and some creatures lull the rest with their notes. The repose is never complete.

This passage, which opens with one of E. B. White's favorite phrases from the book, establishes a sense of place that is more a sensation of place than a concrete locating of it, and this is undoubtedly what White responds to in the paragraph, the feeling that is excited in someone by moving through this particular terrain.

But the chapter that most develops the evocation of specific place is "The Ponds," in which Thoreau figuratively immerses himself in Walden Pond, particularly its waters, and develops a detailed description.

It is a clear and deep green well, half a mile long and a mile and three quarters in circumference, and contains about sixty-one and a half acres; a perennial spring in the midst of pine and oak woods, without any visible inlet or outlet except by the clouds and evaporation. The surrounding hills rise abruptly from the water to the height of forty to eighty feet, though on the south-east and east they attain to about one hundred and one hundred and fifty feet respectively, within a quarter and a third of a mile. They are exclusively woodland.

This is the surveyor in Thoreau speaking, the persona who will later emerge in the chapter "The Ponds in Winter" to include a map of the pond complete with locations for depth soundings and measurements of area, circumference, and length.

It is really in the description of the water that a reader most readily recognizes Thoreau's depth of familiarity with the place as well as his thoroughness of observation.

> Walden is blue at one time and green at another, even from the same point of view. Lying between the earth and the heavens, it partakes of the color of both. Viewed from a hill-top it reflects the color of the sky, but near at hand it is of a yellowish tint next the shore where you can see the sand, then a light green, which gradually deepens to a uniform dark green in the body of the pond. In some lights, viewed even from a hilltop, it is of a vivid green next the shore. Some have referred this to the reflection of the verdure; but it is equally green there against the railroad sand-bank, and in the spring, before the leaves are expanded, and it may be simply the result of the prevailing blue mixed with the yellow of the sand. Such is the color of its iris.

This is by no means a casual account of the color of the water but, rather, a thoughtful examination of it by one who has repeatedly observed the water and contemplated it at length. That thoughtful thoroughness extends to the description of the shore and the distinction Thoreau makes between the impressions a casual onlooker and a close observer have of the pond bottom, shoreline, and plant life.

> The shore is composed of a belt of smooth rounded white stones like paving stones, excepting one or two short sand beaches, and is so steep that in many places a single leap will carry you into water over your head; and were it not for its remarkable transparency, that would be the last to be seen of its bottom till it rose on the opposite shore. Some think it is bottomless. It is nowhere muddy, and a casual observer would say that there were no weeds at all in it; and of noticeable plants, except in the little meadows recently overflowed, which do not properly belong to it, a closer scrutiny does not detect a flag nor a bulrush, nor even a lily, yellow or white, but only a few small heart-leaves and potamogetons, and

perhaps a water-target or two; all which however a bather might not perceive; and these plants are clean and bright like the element they grow in. The stones extend a rod or two into the water, and then the bottom is pure sand, except in the deepest parts, where there is usually a little sediment, probably from the decay of the leaves which have been wafted on to it so many successive falls, and a bright green weed is brought up on anchors even in midwinter.

And it extends to a number of details that the casual visitor might easily overlook or observe without particular notice or curiosity. In talking about the paths around the pond, including no doubt some of the paths on which I too have trodden, he not only notes their presence but also reflects on their origins:

> I have been surprised to detect encircling the pond, even where a thick wood has just been cut down on the shore, a narrow shelf-like path in the steep hill-side, alternately rising and falling, approaching and receding from the water's edge, as old probably as the race of man here, worn by the feet of aboriginal hunters, and still from time to time unwittingly trodden by the present occupants of the land. This is particularly distinct to one standing on the middle of the pond in winter, just after a light snow has fallen, appearing as a clear undulating white line, unobscured by weeds and twigs a quarter of a mile off in many places where in summer it is hardly distinguishable close at hand. The snow reprints it, as it were, in clear white type alto-relievo.

The comparison at the close of the passage is particularly good at making the image come alive for a reader, but it is important to notice that only someone who has been constantly or repeatedly in a certain locale would begin to distinguish features such as this— certainly the hordes of summer visitors would be unaware, and the number of people who have observed this feature from the middle of the pond in winter, even given the frequent harvesting of ice in Thoreau's time and the continued popularity of ice fishing in ours, must be relatively small.

(Walden Pond, Massachusetts)

Thoreau brings to his description of the pond not only his skills as a naturalist and a surveyor but also the advantage of long association with place. Essentially, writers of place are either transients or inhabitants. While perception and reflection and background knowledge may vary from writer to writer regardless of orientation, the advantage always seems—to me, at least, who usually writes as a transient—to lie with the inhabitant. I don't know if memoirs of a year in one place are always more effective than memoirs of a passage through a specific landscape—I like to read (and would like to write) both kinds—but in writing a nonfiction of place the inhabitant seems to have a world of resources to draw on.

Think, for example, of Thoreau's reflection on the changes in water level in Walden Pond over a period of years:

> This rise and fall of Walden at long intervals serves this use at least; the water standing at this great height for a year or more, though it makes it difficult to walk round it, kills the shrubs and trees which have sprung up about its edge since the last rise, pitch pines, birches, alders, aspens, and others, and, falling again, leaves an unobstructed shore; for, unlike many ponds and all waters which are subject to a daily tide, its shore is cleanest when the water is lowest. On the side of the pond next my house, a row of pitch pines fifteen feet high has been killed and tipped over as if by a lever, and thus a stop put to their encroachments; and their size indicates how many years have elapsed since the last rise to this height. By this fluctuation the pond asserts its title to a shore, and thus the *shore* is *shorn*, and the trees cannot hold it by right of possession.

It may well be that a good naturalist, a well-educated ecologist, would make similar observations. Certainly the scientist's training is designed to prepare him or her to make sense of unfamiliar territory, to recognize families of unfamiliar plants or stages in the succession of trees in unfamiliar forests or origins of geological formations in unfamiliar terrain. But that allows chiefly for classification and categorizing, the generalizing of observation. In *Walden* Thoreau is at pains to make sense of his native ground because he dwells in it. Dwelling in it is not only his motive but also his means for making sense of it.

Since the theme of *Walden* is life in the woods at Walden Pond, Thoreau has his entire book to develop the impression of place that permeates it, a somewhat more expansive territory to roam through than White had in a monthly column—it was supposed to take up only four pages in the magazine—or than an essayist generally has. Granted, *Walden* is not only about physical place or about natural history in a specific locale, but nonetheless a sense of place suffuses the entire book—on a certain level, I suppose, the book could be said to be about developing an intensive sensitivity to place—perhaps because a sense of place suffuses the writer.

We sometimes speak about the author's perspective on place in terms of outsider and insider perspectives. The outsider's story is often about discovery, a narrative of entering into landscape and locale and learning either how the sojourner passes through it or how others dwell in it or how to become a dweller in it. The insider's story is often about observation, a narrative of close examination of landscape and locale expressing what time and repetition of experience teach the dweller about place. The insider is an inhabitant, a denizen, a dweller; the outsider is a transient, a traveler, an interloper, in the sense of one loping or simply passing through unfamiliar terrain. The inhabitant's advantage is to be able to let understanding accumulate, to have unasked questions answered almost by osmosis rather than confrontation or direct investigation, to have rehearsed the explanation of experience by thinking or talking about it over time, so that the words that emerge in the writing about place come from a deeper, broader pool of familiarity. The interloper's advantage is to be able to see things afresh, to ask questions that the inhabitant doesn't think to ask because the answers are so familiar as to become transparent, to draw instinctively on experiences of other places in order to understand the one under observation. There are advantages to both intimacy and perspective.

In writing about Walden, Thoreau has the inhabitant's advantage of intimacy, but he also liked to strike out into less familiar territory, as in essays such as "A Walk to Wachusett" and books such as *Cape*

Cod and *The Maine Woods*, to consider what an interloper might discover. E. B. White was certainly familiar with the idea of taking advantage of unfamiliar terrain to get an essay; his visit to Walden is one of several essays in *One Man's Meat* in which he goes off somewhere unfamiliar and writes about his encounters there. The column that he wrote the month before the one on Walden, for example, was about the 1939 New York World's Fair, and the column that appeared two months after the Walden essay was on a camp meeting where Dr. Francis Townsend, a popular lecturer, was speaking. But over the course of the entire *One Man's Meat* collection White establishes himself as a dweller on a saltwater farm, and the book offers a fragmentary approach to the sense of place Thoreau achieved in *Walden*—it was, after all, written as a series of magazine columns rather than a continuous, sequential book. Many of the portions of White's collection have an inhabitant's viewpoint, particularly the pieces on farmwork and community involvement, and over time they make assumptions about the reader's familiarity with setting that an interloper wouldn't make—the transient would feel a need to explain more, and that impulse foregrounds the outsider sensibility. In an essay like "Once More to the Lake" White, ever conscious of his monthly deadline, may have recognized the potential of Great Pond as a subject for an essay like "Walden" or "The World of Tomorrow," but because of his repeated periods of residency at Bear Springs Camp and the relatively unchanging character of the place, he was able to write about it with an inhabitant's knowledge. What "Once More to the Lake" and *Walden* share as nonfiction of place is the writer's deep intimacy with locale over time.

Both writers are conscious of time. As Thoreau memorably observed: "Time is but the stream I go a-fishing in. I drink at it; but while I drink I see the sandy bottom and detect how shallow it is. Its thin current slides away, but eternity remains." Time is also a theme that White returns to, again and again, most memorably in the Great Pond essay and in a later essay called "The Ring of Time" in which a bareback rider rehearses her routine riding around a circus ring and sustains the illusion that time runs around in a circle. Inevitably, during White's visit to Concord, he is conscious of the passage of time, and even as he seems to strain to find timelessness in the technologically advanced society of 1939, he seems aware of the diminished vibrancy of the pond and of Thoreau's worldview. It is Thoreau, however, who provides the window into the past that gives him the chance to glean some perspective on time; without *Walden* White's visit to Concord would be on a par with his visit to the equally unfamiliar World's Fair.

Similarly, without White's essays on Great Pond and Walden Pond and without Thoreau's book, both locations would be terra incognita to me. The curiosity for me is how familiar Great Pond was and how unfamiliar Walden Pond seemed, even from the last time I visited it in 1981. At Great Pond the changes over the sixty-odd years since White wrote his essay seem trivial, not unlike the changes he himself records between his childhood and his son's childhood; time has been moving almost imperceptibly, but the camp, still rustic, with largely the same sorts of recreation, and the lake, still dotted with farms and cottages but not yet overdeveloped, in essence have hardly changed at all. I felt as if I might only have missed White and his son by a matter of hours. At Walden Pond, particularly in the middle of a summer heat wave, the recreational activity, though less raucous perhaps than on Great Pond, overwhelmed the potential serenity of the woodland setting; no matter how much time I spent at the cabin site or on the footpaths, I was never far enough away from vacationing swimmers to get a feeling of isolation. The setting seemed completely remote from Thoreau's experience, in spite of the commemorative signs and posts and cairn of stones.

Thoreau himself dealt with the issue of change at Walden Pond. He claimed, "When I first paddled a boat on Walden, it was completely surrounded by thick and lofty pine and oak woods, and in some of its coves grape vines had run over the trees next the water and formed bowers under which a boat could pass. The hills which form its shores are so steep, and the woods on them were then so high, that, as you looked down from the west end, it had the appearance of an amphitheatre for some kind of sylvan spectacle." He complains, "Now the trunks of trees on the bottom, and the old log canoe, and the dark surrounding woods, are gone, and the villagers, who scarcely know where it lies, instead of going to the pond to bathe or drink, are thinking to bring its water, which should be as sacred as the Ganges at least, to the village in a pipe, to wash their dishes with!—to earn their Walden by the turning of a cock or drawing of a plug!" Yet he still finds that Walden "wears best, and best preserves its purity":

> Though the woodchoppers have laid bare first this shore and then that, and the Irish have built their sties by it, and the railroad has infringed on its border, and the ice-men have skimmed it once, it is itself unchanged, the same water which my youthful eyes fell on; all the change is in me. ... It struck me again tonight, as if I had not seen it almost daily for more than twenty years,—Why, here is Walden, the same woodland lake that I discovered so many years ago; where a forest was cut down last winter another is springing up by its shore as lustily as ever; the same thought is welling up to its surface that was then; it is the same liquid joy and happiness to itself and its Maker, ay, and it *may* be to me.

Thoreau is endeavoring to sort out what is time bound and what is timeless, what is mutable and what is immutable, at Walden Pond, in a way that prefigures White's reflections on the same themes at Great Pond. There White's final recognition of the inevitability of change—of death—is mitigated by the sameness of the essence of the place itself ("It was all the same"). The change, as it is for Thoreau, is in him, not in the place, or, more importantly, in the power the place has to evoke a connectedness to something more timeless and enduring than mere human existence.

At bottom, then, the essence of a nonfiction of place is its ability to capture that connectedness and convey it to another person, the reader who gets to be virtual inhabitant or interloper through the pages of the text. Thoreau can convey that sense about Walden, and White can convey that sense about Great Pond, but because my connection to either place is only through these writers (as White's is to Walden), my understanding can only be measured in terms of how much I recognize or fail to recognize of the earlier author's sense of place during my own time there. My vision is filtered through the optics of the prisms they provide for me. How much of what I see of Great Pond or of Walden Pond is an accurate vision of the place itself rather than of the place as another writer has seen it? What would I make of Walden if the memorial to Thoreau's cabin weren't there? If I could see Walden without the intervening scrim of Thoreau's account, how much would my sense of place align with his? Even then, I doubt whether my bystander's perspective on Walden would be sufficient to convey the sense of place that Thoreau's dweller perspective has made so enduring.

Walden 2002

> This was one of the *great* days; though the sky had from my clearing only that everlastingly great look that it wears daily, and I saw no difference in it.
> —HENRY THOREAU, *Walden*

I knew I would go once more to the pond before I left, and the clouds I noticed outside the restaurant decided me to go that evening. I had eaten at a good Mediterranean restaurant in the Concord Depot, with an eastern view of the parking lot and the Amtrak trains passing through and disembarking passengers and the people waiting for the passengers on the trains and a walker crossing the train tracks talking on a cell phone. I had made my last bookshop purchase, was enjoying my final meal in Concord, and had draped a sense of leave-taking around me like the heavy cloak of humidity that had dogged the day.

So, when I stepped up to the car, keys in hand, and saw the western sky, I did a double take. It was past six-thirty, and the sun was lowering itself, but a distinctive blue-gray cloud roughly the shape of Australia had gotten between the sun and the earth, and another had slid between that cloud and the sun, and a golden outline clung to the borders of the clouds and radiated outward into blue sky. I thought what this must look like over the pond and reflected in its waters and hastily drove out there. It was around seven when I set off along the pond path, dipping onto the shoreline for a short stretch but mostly staying just above it.

I reached the site of the hut and stepped up to the cairn to deposit a stone I'd picked up on the beach, to add to the stones of Whitman and White and countless others. A couple and their teenaged son approached as I positioned the stone. I wanted to have a little more time alone at the site, so I retreated to my familiar stump to wait them out. The father, standing on the far side of the pillars from the cairn, pitched a pebble on the pile with a smirk; the boy walked his little stone over and dropped it, a compromise between pilgrim values and his father's. As they went off, another couple intent on the beach emerged from the woods and passed through the clearing without seeming to notice it.

Left alone at the site, I had the sense that I was taking leave of Thoreau, and then it struck me that when I had spoken to the dead in Maine, it was at E. B. White's grave in Brooklin, not at the camp on Great Pond. Thoreau rests in Sleepy Hollow Cemetery, and there's the place for leave-taking, but it seemed to me that, in spite of the bathing paradise beyond the trees, Henry's spirit is still in the woods (or at least that's where I imagined it). It seemed paradoxical that, in Thoreau's case, a writer's sense of place could have vanished from a locale without his spirit accompanying it or that, in White's case, a writer's sense of place could have endured while his spirit had departed. In literature a writer's sense of place and a writer's presence in the text may be inextricably linked, but when we visit those locations in life, either the sense of place or the writer's presence—or both—may be impossible to locate.

I set off again to complete my final circuit of the pond, sauntering above the shoreline until I reached Long Cove, then tramping on the beach like everyone else. The water was silvery blue against the darkening trees, and die-hard bathers showed mostly just their heads, dark lumps in the gleaming pond, not so much swimming as treading water or, more often, placidly sitting on the shallow bottom along the shore. As soon as I was a little way down the south shore, away from the western border of trees, I could see the clouds again, now changed, darker but still with gleaming edges and openings of bright light and the sky where there was no sun or cloud a deepening even blue. It was a sky with that great everlasting look that Thoreau and White refer to, the kind of sky the Hudson River School painters were so adept at capturing. Darkness was falling, and the reservation was closing, but on my way back to my car I kept looking over my shoulder all around the shoreline to catch sight through the trees of that everlastingly great sky.

Here Is New York
(New York, New York)

i.

March 19, 2003. We have been told to arrive early at Detroit Metro for our flight to New York City because the enhanced security measures will lengthen the time it takes to get to the boarding gate, but once at the new terminal, and with only a little help from an airline agent, it doesn't take long for my colleague John and me to print out our e-tickets, check our bags, and clear the security check at our concourse. Once past the dour and ominous security officers, we find ourselves drifting through the terminal with an unexpected amount of time to spend before our flight. We idle away some of it with a superfluous cup of coffee and disinterested browsing, then find our gate, where the waiting area is already filling, and settle into low seats to await the boarding call.

Behind us a giant television screen fills much of the wall at our end of the waiting area. The old terminal had plenty of TVs blaring a twenty-four-hour news channel, but they had been small and possible to evade; in the new terminal the screens are gigantic, visible from yards and yards away, and unavoidable. We sit with our backs to the screen deliberately, but passengers on their way to other gates stop in the passages alongside the moving walk to check up on events, and we are constantly aware of a shifting throng of people edging toward us, their faces upturned and glum.

This morning the news channels are reporting, with that urgency and earnestness that dramatizes their own seriousness of purpose and implies a vital importance to what they show, the last-minute preparations for our next war. They run banners under talking heads and repetitious film clips announcing either the "Showdown in Iraq" or the "Showdown with Saddam," as if the Texan in Washington and the Muslim in Baghdad were equally matched gunslingers and the eventual outcome were not in doubt. Elsewhere in the terminal we saw headlines across the front page of *USA Today* trumpeting the news that both the Delta Force and the CIA have been training for months to kill the president of Iraq, pictured farther down the page like a mustachioed villain of wild west wanted posters. Like Alfredo Garcia, Pancho Villa, Joaquín Murietta—bring me the head of Saddam Hussein. No one seems to be questioning the treatment of assassination by Americans as a spectator sport. On TV the Texan, who has been a-hankerin' for this fight for months, is repeatedly shown mouthing some "A man's gotta do what a man's gotta do" sound bite, to the apparent approval, or at least indifference or possibly eagerness, of members of the media, all of whom remember what his father's Gulf War did for CNN's ratings.

I doggedly put my head down and try to concentrate on the book I've brought to read on the flight. Sometimes my most concentrated periods of reading are before and during flights. Because of the noise of the crowd around me and the low volume of the television, I'm able to miss most of what's being reported but still find my consciousness floating above the surface of the text.

Once airborne, I continue to read but can't help overhearing some of John's conversation with the woman in the window seat. Together they ponder the effect of the imminent invasion on air travel, speculate on the nervousness about events that makes some people think themselves imprudent if they don't hunker down like Iraqis awaiting the bombs. I am introverted and John extroverted, and our respective behaviors are predictably typical of our personality types, but I also detect beneath his gregariousness the intermittent compulsion to air his anxieties and confront them in the transparent guise of casual conversation. For both him and the woman talking seems to build up pressure and stress and simultaneously to vent and relieve it.

The flight is not long, and soon we are descending for our approach to La Guardia. From my aisle seat I try to see past the two of them for views of New York City. In spite of my cynicism about the war, my sense of helplessness about the downward spiral of democracy under this president, I know that somewhere below us is a gaping hole where the World Trade Towers stood until September 11, 2001. I can't help thinking of the hijacked planes whose impact brought the towers down and of the people in them, just like us, who had approached the city as we approach it. Given the nearly global opposition to the invasion of Iraq and the shifty justifications behind it, coming events seem certain to further inflame anti-American feelings and further incite suicidal berserkers. Looking down on the city with the memory of recent horror and the certainty of more in the future, I find it easy to mistake the blue-gray haze over Manhattan for a pall.

We land, take a cab to the Edison, and check in. In the lobby we run into another colleague from our department. Susan tells us that, because of the coming war, her husband insisted that she change her flight plans and come home a day early. She will see little of the conference or the city. I propose we get a drink at the Algonquin Hotel, a few blocks away, and the three of us set off in afternoon sunshine. In Times Square headlines curling across the buildings tickertape the impending war, and people on the street move haltingly, trying to read and walk at the same time and not bump into those who simply stop and gape upward. A crowd of young people lines the curb outside the MTV studio; among them is a teenaged girl holding a placard on which she claims to be related to Michelle Branch, a popular singer possibly now inside the building, and demands to be admitted. None of the MTV crowd turns toward the headlines scrolling above Times Square.

We wander into the Algonquin Hotel and gaze on the group portrait of the Round Table crowd on the wall, a painting as big as a TV screen at the Detroit airport, and while we each sip a single malt scotch at our little round table, repeating a convention ritual the three of us have created, we talk only about New York literary life and campus politics and upcoming conference events. Later we meet a friend of

Susan's in publishing and make an evening of it—dinner at Pong-sai, a Thai place on Forty-Eighth; a drink at Hurley's, another historic watering hole; a nightcap at Joe Allen's on Forty-Sixth—talking all the while about publishing and Susan's friend's career and pleasant common ground.

At Joe Allen's a little TV perches above the door, and at 10:15 the president appears on the screen to declare that the "disarming" of Iraq has begun—a man of many euphemisms, he earlier spoke of "eliminating the security threat to America" rather than "conquering a foreign country," and his tagline for the invasion, "Operation Iraqi Freedom," has a nobler ring to it than his father's more macho "Operation Desert Storm." Luckily, the bar is noisy enough to drown him out if you don't stand directly below the TV, but continual close-ups of the smirking commander-in-chief remind us how long the day has been and how long the next days will be, and we leave Susan's friend in the bar to return to the hotel.

Earlier, leaving Hurley's and turning east toward Broadway, we saw the moon through the gap between the buildings in their best "skyscraper" pose on either side of Forty-Eighth Street. The moon was opalescent and full, gleaming in a placid blue-black sky lightly laced with thin, transparent clouds. It made the world seem beautiful and serene above the bustle of this scarred and still vibrant city. I look again for the image of that brilliant moon and tranquil sky as we walk back to the Edison. I try to conjure that image behind my eyelids as I fall asleep.

ii.

The visit to the Algonquin wasn't simply a pilgrimage to the site of the famous Roundtable, where wits like Robert Benchley, Dorothy Parker, George Kauffmann, and others had gathered in the 1920s. I'd always wanted to have a cocktail there, perhaps because it was the kind of place where a small-town boy like me could use the word *cocktail* unselfconsciously. But it was only after rereading E. B. White's *Here Is New York* a few days earlier, to get in a New York state of mind, that I'd promised myself I'd stop by. White had stayed there in the summer of 1948 while he was researching that essay, originally published in 1949, for *Holiday Magazine*, where his stepson Roger Angell was an editor. Published as a small book later the same year, it remains an enduring literary snapshot of the city.

I especially like the moments when White sets off to stroll around the city. "I wander around, re-examining this spectacle, hoping that I can put it on paper," he says. He saunters down West Forty-Eighth Street, listening to music in the parlors and watching the behavior of a matinee audience as they empty a theater and encounter a street singer. He takes in the other diners at a former speakeasy on East Fifty-Third, a concert in the Mall in Central Park, the view from his office windows on a Saturday afternoon, the view from a café on Ninth Street. He walks the Bowery past the homeless under the El at night, heads east along Rivington through the slums and tenements, observes an open-air dance in a playground on Lewis. He hears the horn of the Queen Mary at its dock. He appreciates how much the city has changed in his lifetime (he grew up in nearby Mount Vernon and had lived regularly or intermittently in the city for over twenty-five years by the time he wrote this essay) and even how much it has changed in the months between the magazine version and the book version. As one example of almost instantaneous change, he says in the book's foreword, "The Lafayette Hotel, mentioned in passing, has passed in spite of the mention," and then he claims, "To bring New York down to date, a man would have to be published with the speed of light." He writes that it is the reader's duty to bring New York down to date and "trust[s] it will prove less a duty than a pleasure."

In the dimly lit recesses in the back of my mind, where I store the uncertain and improbable intentions I don't want to admit to other people, I thought I might bring New York down to date for myself while I was in town. In the front of my mind, hurtling around like moths in a lighted closet, were obligations to a panel presentation, a roundtable discussion, a board meeting with a group of colleagues at a midtown apartment, a dinner with different colleagues, a publisher's reception and another publisher's party, and some time manning a booth in an exhibit hall as well. Add to these expectations of impromptu networking and occasionally hearing conference presentations by other people. Nowhere in my mind was an awareness that I would have only sixty-seven hours between initial arrival at the hotel and final departure, from which would be subtracted roughly eighteen to twenty-four hours of sleep, in which to do all this.

Not surprisingly, I didn't get out much on my own.

Leaving a Thursday morning meeting at an apartment on Seventy-Second just east of Second Avenue, I found myself alone under the building's sidewalk canopy, suddenly released into the city. Instead of flagging down a cab, as I'd intended, I strode off in a light rain down Second Avenue. I thought this was my chance to saunter and observe, but the drizzle continued, and I walked briskly, trying to avoid puddles and feeling the rain soak my hair and my shoulders and seep into my shoes, and the street, mostly made up of blocks of restaurants and small shops, made little lasting impression on me. At Forty-Eighth Street I splashed east toward First Avenue in search of Turtle Bay Gardens, where a willow tree in the garden of White's apartment building had been the final image of *Here Is New York*, both in White's prose and in a drawing by Edward C. Caswell. In a December 2002 article in the *New York Times* Steve Dougherty had revisited the tree and found it still standing; it was a kind of landmark location for me, one I'd long hoped to visit. In the end I thought I might have passed it—a series of row houses with the tree and the garden hidden from street view—but wasn't positive. And the rain persisted.

Weary of walking, of being wet and cold, I stepped into Devon & Blakely, on Forty-Seventh near Lexington, to get hot coffee, soak up some of the rain in my hair with a handful of napkins, and ponder what I was accomplishing. Outside the window where I sat, the world was busily in motion, traffic heavy on the streets, New Yorkers bustling along the sidewalks. Everyone was intent on something, crossing the street, dancing around pools of water, dodging each other, dialing cell phones. They all seemed to have destinations and the determination to achieve them. In the coffee shop I overheard conversations about dating; childcare; and the joy of lying on a couch, drinking beer, and watching television ("It's better than sex," one of the twenty-something men enthused). Within the café lines of people shuffled past the counters getting coffee and sandwiches to go. It seemed like a typical Thursday in the city, bustling and busy and energetic, and no one seemed to have the war news in mind. Inspired by so many people purposefully in motion, I finished my coffee and stepped briskly back into the rain, heading toward Fifty-Third and Sixth Avenue, where the convention was, so that I too could seem purposeful.

I angled up toward the conference, a block west, then two blocks north, then another block or two west, until I recognized the spires of St. Patrick's Cathedral and veered in its direction. On Fifty-First Street I entered the south side of the cathedral up near the altar. St. Patrick's was busy too. Tourists were milling around, gaping at walls and windows and the vaulting of the roof, and in the nave a tour group was being lectured to as their guide led them toward the altar. Some people slumped in pews seemed be homeless New Yorkers seeking respite from a cold rain, but I noted a scattering of others sitting glumly or kneeling at prayer. I wondered how many were thinking about the war, praying for its speedy resolution now that it had begun, praying for safe return of our troops or safe haven for Iraqi noncombatants or both. Perhaps it had been the war and not tourism or rain that had brought me into the cathedral as well. Taking their example, I slid into an empty pew and sat down.

I stared ahead at the altar but didn't really see it. I thought for a moment about how I alternate between fury and despair over what I see as the steady decline of the country, then found myself wishing that something like hope or calm might catch up with me. I knew before I sat down that I'm not really capable of belief or prayer, but I'd like to be capable of peace or momentary tranquillity, and St. Patrick's seemed as good a place as any to give it a try. My gaze drifted upward, toward the ceiling of the nave. Arranged in rows above the congregation were two sets of flags, those of the United States and the Vatican. Seeming to jointly celebrate unity in obedience and faith in infallibility, they helped to keep my thoughts earthbound. When I looked around at other people in the pews, I hoped that some of them were praying, no matter how futilely, for our troops and for their victims and for reason and compassion to triumph, just once, over cruelty and self-righteousness. For myself I had to get out of the cathedral. I knew I would be better off back out in the rain.

I wandered wearily back to the conference and walled out the city with panels, publishers' parties, presentations, professional chatter. It was the convention routine I usually get caught up in, but I felt distracted and disengaged, as if I were merely flying on automatic pilot. Even outside the convention, in the occasional passage between the hotel on Forty-Seventh between Seventh and Eighth and the conference at Fifty-Third and Sixth, I felt cut off from the city.

The war news saturated the media, as if there were no other news, and in New York media saturates the environment. Televisions run endlessly, even in the cabs and on the elevators as well as in the bars and restaurants. On Sixth Avenue Fox News headquarters scrolled headlines in huge letters around the building, and Times Square was ablaze with similar images. Nowhere did there seem to be news channel–free zones. Even the Weather Channel, the only channel I watched in my room, reported the weather in Iraq.

On Friday night, passing near Times Square and crossing Broadway on the way back to our hotel, we saw crowds of young people milling around and a heavy concentration of police. Neon and celebrity images and shifting lights and an amalgam of music and traffic sounds and voices created a festive, almost frantic atmosphere throughout the area. So many perpetually altering electronic billboards and flashing lights bombarded the eye that it was hard to distinguish one from another. It didn't seem to matter what the noises and images were about—they weren't supposed to mean but simply be. Maybe that was why the war news seemed to have so little impact, because it was only another variation in endlessly morphing walls of sight and sound, no more meaningful than the vegetarian actress naked beneath lettuce leaves on one of the brightest billboards, no more capable of holding the miniscule span of the public attention. Maybe I hadn't been cut off from the city—maybe the city had been cut off from itself, transmographied into an unending media barrage.

When I looked out between our curtains in the middle of the night, the reversed image of the gigantic, ever-changing, blinking and mutating soft drink ad that runs twenty-four hours a day on the building next to ours was reflected in the windows of the hotel across the street. It was all I could see of the city.

iii.

March 22. Our day of departure, the morning sky bright and sunny after two gray days of intermittent drizzle and downpour. The war goes on. A massive antiwar demonstration is planned for midday in Times Square, and we leave especially early to avoid traffic snarls, an unnecessary precaution. A bad accident blocks traffic in the freeway lanes heading toward Manhattan and backs up cars for miles, but our cab ride to La Guardia takes us to the airport in light traffic. In the airport, with a couple hours to spend waiting, we check in and check through security and sit with other colleagues at the gate for the flight to Detroit. Two of our friends tell us they took time off from the conference for some sightseeing, and one of the places they went was the site of the World Trade Center, Ground Zero on 9/11, as we tend to call it. They are surprised not to be more moved by the site itself, scene of so much horror and rage and, temporarily, a binding national grief. They expected upwellings of some of those emotions when they gazed into the crater where the city's tallest buildings had been, but it had little impact on them. One of them says, "It looks mostly just like a massive construction site." The flow of commerce creates similar sites every year; perhaps the Lafayette Hotel created such a crater, on a somewhat smaller scale, when they demolished it to build a skyscraper in its place.

E. B. White's *Here Is New York* ends with a section on "the stubborn fact of annihilation" in which he gave gruesome hints of what might happen in an air attack: "The city, for the first time in its long history, is destructible. A single flight of planes no bigger than a wedge of geese can quickly end this island fantasy, burn the towers, crumble the bridges, turn the underground passages into lethal chambers, cremate the millions. The intimation of mortality is part of New York now: in the sound of jets overhead, in the black headlines of the latest edition." World War II was over, and Germany had been reduced to rubble, and Hiroshima and Nagasaki had been obliterated, and the debris of war was still spread across Europe. The Cold War had begun, and the menacing memory of the atomic cloud hung heavy over the planet. White's scenario was merely grim speculation in his day, but since the destruction of the World Trade Center, it has felt uncomfortably like prophecy.

White also pointed out that at the same time, not far from Turtle Bay Gardens, where he and his wife kept an apartment, the United Nations Building was under construction, to house an international congress of diplomats and to explore the belief that if enough nations were united in the cause of peace, it might be possible to maintain. White observed that there was "a race between the destroying planes and the struggling Parliament of Man" and thought that "the city at last perfectly illustrates both the universal dilemma and the general solution . . . the perfect target and the perfect demonstration of nonviolence." In the intervening half-century he has seemed overly optimistic.

Flying into La Guardia a few days ago, viewing the city from the air again, I thought of White's fear for the city and the way that terrorists had confirmed it. Now, leaving from La Guardia three days later, while television channels were proudly displaying images of aerial attacks by our military on Baghdad, I think: The destroying planes outracing the Parliament of Man are ours; the chance for peace is being evaded by us; our government drops the stubborn fact of annihilation on a foreign city, its people the victims, we the aggressor.

A slight haze hangs above the city, but I can see virtually the whole

Here Is New York

of Manhattan, a flat, level, gray island surrounded by the shimmering waters of the Hudson and the East River and the harbor. Though I have been at its center, surrounded by its nearly unbelievable complexity and intricacy, walking through the middle of its immense scale, from the air it seems very open, very small, very vulnerable. From this perspective it seems more destructible than it has ever been, indistinguishable in that regard from all the other cities of the world.

three

Anasazi
(The Four Corners)

I am haunted by the ghosts of the Anasazi, the ancient ones of the Mesa Verde cliff dwellings, the Chaco Canyon pueblos, and thousands of other sites scattered across the Four Corners. I am haunted by the spirits of those who peopled the Cliff Palace, Pueblo Bonito, the primitive pit houses on Chapin Mesa, and the Great Kiva of Casa Rinconada. Once I gazed at a stark, sheer wall of Cliff Canyon only to discover the shattered ruins of an Anasazi house secreted in a niche under a massive overhang—saw it emerging in my vision like a spirit photograph; now I browse coffee table books of western landscape photography half-expecting to discover in the scenery a telltale set of handholds in rock overhangs, props beneath great boulders, the remnants of a wall, or the outline of a buried kiva. Like buildings taking sudden shape upon a bare canyon wall or a city of clay and stone rising from a desolate desert, the Anasazi seem to be just beyond my vision, perhaps drawn back down the Great Sipapu from which in the beginning mankind first emerged, and I am haunted by a sense of their imminent presence.

That August Sue and I had crammed clothing, camping gear, and all kinds of guidebooks into a Chevette and left Missouri for the Southwest, first sweltering through the prairie heat of Kansas and then steaming through the mountain rain of southern Colorado. Yet when we turned off us 160 between Mancos and Cortez onto the road to Mesa Verde National Park, we were not too weary to be startled by the flat cylinder of rock rising from the pine forest. We drove cautiously up the steep, winding entrance road carved out of the side of the mesa, two lowland midwesterners both awed and unnerved by the tortuous twists and turns, the magnificent view unfolding ever farther below us, the sheer drop seeming always to be only inches away.

Morfield Campground, located in a basin surrounded by further heights of the mesa, had over five hundred campsites, but each campsite was isolated from the others by pinyon pine and juniper and tall grass. When we began setting up the tent, the only ones who watched us were a mule deer doe and her twins, kibitzing at the border of the trees. Near sunset, dozens of deer slipped out to browse in the high grass; campers strolling around the campground in the fading light stopped in the road to watch them, and the deer stared back warily while they ate.

The night turned cool, and the campground quieted, and the sky was clear and dazzlingly brilliant with stars. We found our way to the campground amphitheater to listen to a talk on astronomy. One of the park rangers had set up a telescope and helped us locate Mars, Jupiter, four of Jupiter's moons, and some constellations. On our return the lights of lanterns and wood fires were absorbed by the surrounding vegetation, and the campground seemed sparsely populated, even though we knew it was nearly full. We were only aware of that dazzling overcrowded sky, for the first time in our lives appearing before us unobstructed, in its full glory. We fell asleep looking up at that dense canopy of stars, feeling absolutely alone except for the company of the universe.

In the morning we drove off toward the ruins. Mesa Verde, the "green table" aptly named by early Spanish-speaking visitors to the region, spreads out to the south in long peninsulas separated by deep, narrow canyons. The Anasazi ruins most visitors see are on Chapin Mesa, some sixteen miles south of the campground. There, at Mesa Top Ruins, the neatly laid out archaeological evidence follows the path of development that culminated in the magnificent cliff dwellings built in the twelfth century CE and abandoned mysteriously soon after. The peoples who wandered onto Mesa Verde from unknown origins around 600 CE were Modified Basket Makers. They found in the climate of the mesa a place to develop their agriculture of corn and squash and supplemented it by hunting the plentiful game with spears, using an atlatl, or spear thrower, for greater force. Mesa Verde rises seven to eight thousand feet above sea level; its rains are more plentiful than in the surrounding area, and the Anasazi soon learned how to capitalize on the rainfall by building abundant dams and irrigation channels—the remains of Mummy Lake, one of their reservoirs, is still visible at Far View Ruins.

In time their population grew. At first they built pit houses by excavating earthen circles, strengthening the walls, and covering it all with a raised roof of sticks and wattle. The entrance was through the smoke hole on the roof. Originally pit houses were single-family dwellings and single rooms; eventually, anterooms were added for storage. Then, as the population grew, the pit houses were replaced by pueblos, multiroom dwellings built above ground of single-course masonry, a row of stones mortared with mud. The pit house, which had been not only a dwelling place but a place of ceremonial events, survived in the communal kiva, a large circular pit whose common elements included a fire pit in the center, supporting pilasters or pillars, a banquette, or bench, encircling the room, niches in the wall for ceremonial objects, and a ladder leading to the roof by which clan members entered or exited. Ventilation shafts were added to bring in fresh air by another source than the smoke hole / entrance, and a stone slab was added to deflect the airflow and circulate it around the room. Each kiva also had a small circular hole in the floor, the *sipapu*, a symbolic reminder of the Great Sipapu, the hole in the earth leading to the underworld from which, according to myth, mankind first appeared in this world.

The development from pit house to pueblo was a matter of centuries, a time of growing population, stable and increasing food supply, and expanding trade with other Indian cultures. From the world outside Mesa Verde came beans, a more reliable crop; the improved hunting technology of the bow and arrow; pottery, which the Anasazi adopted and enhanced with their own unique black-and-white designs; and better techniques of construction, apparently developed in the pueblos of the Chaco culture to the south.

The Chaco culture had developed in ways similar to Mesa Verde throughout the same period. Chaco Canyon, in west central New Mexico, is a broad desert rimmed with low mesas. There the Anasazi developed an extensive culture of interrelated towns and outposts. Roads were developed, trade routes established, lookout towers constructed with some system of communication between outposts and central pueblos. At the center was Pueblo Bonito, an enormous planned city of over six hundred rooms and thirty-three kivas, terraced up to five stories high and supporting an estimated population of a thousand people. The desert Anasazi had an influence on the Anasazi of Mesa Verde, particularly in the method of stone construction of pueblos, and the trade between them must have been vigorous.

But in the twelfth century, almost at the height of their prosperity, the Chaco Anasazi abandoned Pueblo Bonito and vanished, their extensive culture withered, and their buildings were left to the ravages of time. And at Mesa Verde the Anasazi began to construct their dwellings in sandstone overhangs on canyon walls, leaving the mesa tops for the cultivation of crops but living their lives in cliff dwellings that sometimes reached astonishing size. They came and went from the dwellings by means of hand and toeholds scraped in the sheer cliff face, descending a hundred feet from the rim to buildings often perched hundreds of feet above the canyon floor. It was a precarious, if well protected, existence.

And then, at the end of the century, following twenty-three years of drought, dated by tree ring dendrochronology as 1276–99, the mountain Anasazi too disappeared, abandoned their cliff dwellings, left no traces of where they went. When nomadic tribes such as the Utes, the Navajos, and the Apaches wandered into the region, they avoided the deserted buildings. Today the Ute reservation surrounds Mesa Verde on three sides, and the Navajo reservation to the west of Chaco Canyon occupies an area larger than New England stretching across New Mexico, Arizona, and Utah, much of it dotted with Anasazi ruins.

There are mysteries here, about both the origins of the Anasazi and their fate and about the decisions they made concerning the culture they created in the five centuries in which their culture is recorded. The pueblos and cliff dwellings seem to be defensive measures, particularly the double-course masonry that replaced simpler construction in later centuries, but there is no historical evidence of warfare or invaders—the known nomadic tribes came much later. We understand little about the relationship between such towns as Pueblo Bonito and Cliff Palace and their outlying communities and outposts. What little we assume about the religious and ceremonial activities in the kivas we interpolate from studying modern Pueblo ceremonies—surely the Anasazi were the ancestors of the modern Pueblo peoples, though shifts of population among ancient Indian peoples are not so simply explained as that. One interpretation of their demise sees it as an ecological warning, an example of how overpopulation and counterproductive agricultural practices can leave a culture with no means of survival; the counterargument is that twenty-five years of drought surely would wreak more havoc on a primitive agriculture than the devastation wrought on a more advanced agriculture in the few short years that created the twentieth century dustbowl. Moreover, Chaco was deserted before the great drought at Mesa Verde began, while the rain was still falling.

These are issues we may never resolve. The Anasazi left only abstract designs and some few petroglyphs—no written language, no hieroglyphics or cuneiform tablets, no Rosetta stone. And yet we still can feel their presence in the cliff dwellings of Mesa Verde.

The white man's first significant encounter with the cliff dwellings of Mesa Verde occurred just over a hundred years ago, on December 18, 1888, when two drovers hunting in the snow for lost cattle happened deep into one of the canyons outlining the mesa and discovered, in a single day, the ruins we now call Spruce Tree House, Square Tower House, and the Cliff Palace. The modern traveler sometimes recaptures that experience by standing on the rim of the mesa, taking in the stark beauty of one of its canyons, measuring the plunge to the canyon floor, slowly surveying the kaleidoscopic changes in rugged grandeur along its walls, and then, suddenly, realizing that among the sandstone shapes, tucked into a long, narrow niche, shadowed in part by the massive stone overhang and perched impossibly in the midst of a sheer rock face, are a series of stone walls, perhaps the telltale shape of a window or doorway. He squints and focuses on the sandstone-colored ruin, searching in vain for a discernible path or road to the building, and turns to tell his wife. But when he looks once more, the harsh sunlight disguises the building again; as he scours the ledges and overhangs, the dark lines and shadowy openings, he seems to find it suddenly but farther south than he remembered and somehow missing a wall or two. His wife has meanwhile found a ruin herself, this one north of where he began pointing, and as he follows her arm, he rediscovers the first ruin and almost simultaneously sights the third one, the one she had found.

One of them is well preserved, perhaps restored in part by the National Park Service, and well protected by a large overhang; the ledge it sits upon seems level and secure. Another is an eroding remnant of a building of several rooms; over the centuries the ledge to which it clings obviously has broken away as far back as the very center of the house itself, perhaps carried down into the canyon by the fall of a portion of the cliff face that had overhung the house originally— lines of fracture are still visible on the rock above the building. The condition of the third is somewhere in between the other two, still secure on the cliff face but crumbled and hobbled by its own debris. And even as he marvels aloud that buildings could be constructed on ledges seemingly inaccessible to mountain goats, he discerns the regularly spaced indentations in the cliff face that mark the handholds the Anasazi used to descend to those buildings, and he feels a thrill of acrophobia run through him.

In such a discovery the visitor replicates the surprise of those two cowboys a century ago, an unnerving realization that these steep rocky canyons harbor the ghosts of a culture long vanished. Often, having turned away from the view of the canyon, the visitor has to search again to find the cliff dwellings. Standing on the rim of the mesa, just off the modern blacktop road that winds through Gambel oak and thick dry grasses, he may feel a sense of isolation on his side of the canyon, until he discovers that nearby the National Park Service has installed a stairway down the canyon wall and that a hundred feet directly below him, unheard and unseen, dozens of campers and day visitors like him are scrambling among ruins more extensive than those he searches for in the distance.

We descended to the Cliff Palace on such a stairway, twisting its way down the cliff face and threading through fractures and around debris, now a man-made series of steps, then a footpath along a ledge. The approach allows a panoramic view of the Cliff Palace, and the result is awesome. Under a massive lowering brow of rock stand the remnants of a prehistoric city of interconnected apartments, terraces, towers, and pits. At its most extensive it had had over 217 rooms and 23 kivas and an estimated population of 200 to 250 people. Deep within the overhang a ledge, now inaccessible, shelters walls where food was stored; entrance would have been gained by means of a ladder on the roof of a four-story building, now no longer so high. Much of the Cliff Palace is similarly gone, the debris cleared for visitors, some walls restored or repaired in the Anasazi manner, but the general sense of the place remains. Here was a city of streets and plazas, private dwellings and communal buildings, all tightly linked together and demanding a complicated sense of social order.

We moved along the terraces, gazing through T-shaped doorways at dark square rooms, peering into the kivas where clans met to carry on the ceremonies that were responsible for keeping the Anasazi in harmony with the universe. Where walls had fallen and roofs collapsed, we could see the quality of construction, the overlapping of stone and mud mortar, the bracing up with wooden beams.

From an upper terrace we could look down into one of the open kivas. At Spruce Tree House, another ruin, we had been allowed to descend into a kiva with its roof intact. We had felt the coolness of the semidarkness, the overarching weight of the roof and the mesa above—it had made us feel for a moment closer to the underworld. Sitting on a bench built into the wall, gazing around the kiva, we had heard the bustle of people outside and begun to imagine it was the bustle of Anasazi society. Then we had emerged into sunlight and summer warmth and the twentieth century, into the viewfinders of European and Asian and American photographers and a babel of conversation. At Cliff Palace, gazing into the open kiva, it wasn't hard to imagine these buildings restored and active.

The climb out of the canyon, by another way than the path in, was steep and tiring but gradual and safe, nothing like the hand-over-hand scramble up the rock face the Anasazi had faced daily to ascend to the agriculture of the mesa top or descend to the springs at the base of the canyon. Our climb gave us yet another panorama of the Cliff Palace, gleaming in the sun, and yet when we turned to look back a few feet farther up, it was gone, and behind us the canyon seemed silent and empty.

Throughout our stay we wandered the ruins of Chapin Mesa, often descending arduously to investigate features of various dwellings. We strolled the mesa rim searching for inaccessible sites nearly invisible in both glaring sunlight and shadow and occasionally clambered across the walls of mesa top ruins like the Sun Temple or Far View Pueblo. Once we drove to Park Point, around eighty-six hundred feet above sea level, nearly two thousand feet above the rest of the mesa, four thousand feet above the surrounding Delores Plateau from which the mesa rises. The view extends for 360 degrees, to the easily identified figure of Sleeping Ute Mountain in the West and the Delores Peaks and Mount Wilson in the North, across the Mancos Valley to the East, toward the singular volcanic shape of Shiprock in the South. The unaided eye could barely discern the sparse sprinkling of communities in the lowlands, and the distances were great enough that it was easy to believe that the world beyond Mesa Verde was unpopulated, that the tent and rv dwellers of the Morfield Campground were somehow the last outpost of the Anasazi, taking refuge on the overgrown mesa, while the buildings of the ancient ones continued to crumble and those of the less ancient ones we had fled had already begun to decay.

One evening, because I hadn't had enough of that magnificent view, I walked alone from the campground out the Knife Edge Trail to watch the sunset over the Montezuma Valley. A modern road had once extended along the western cliff face of the mesa, but the farther you walked, the more evidence you found of how the mesa had rejected it, like an incompatible transplanted organ. Massive boulders littered the road from above, and the eroded cliff face had torn away chunks of it from below until the road itself disappeared into the earth. The sun sank behind Sleeping Ute Mountain, its glow incarnadining the mesa wall and casting its craggy face into red relief. I watched it as long as I could, then started back before the absolute darkness of the mesa night could catch me on the trail.

As usual, the mule deer were moving in the thickets and rustling through the undergrowth on the bluff above the trail. Rounding a boulder, I surprised a trio—a buck with the downy beginnings of antlers and two young does—on the trail and tried to pass them casually, without putting them to flight. All three watched me for a moment without moving, then bolted for the bluff. I was startled by their sudden movement but continued on my way until I heard a sound behind me. Turning, I saw the young buck following me cautiously. My movement sent him toward the bluff again, but he clearly had no intention of dashing into hiding. Instead, he took a parallel route halfway up the rise, made his way ahead of me, and then stopped, watching me all the while. Behind me, visible but safe at the top of the bluff, the two does watched us. Expecting skittishness, I was unsettled by the buck's belligerence. I started walking again, keeping one eye on the buck and the other on the uncertain footing of the trail. He moved parallel with me, his progress on the loose shale noisy and often graceless, until a boulder in his path made him pause. I continued along the trail around it and heard him come down to the slope to level ground. Voices drifted up from ahead of me on the trail. I stopped and looked back at the mule deer. He stopped and kept his head low. In the faint gleam in his eyes I thought I could see the spirit of a powerful stag with a full rack, but he seemed satisfied that he had escorted me out of his neighborhood—when I went off toward the campground, he stayed behind. In the dimmer light away from the western rim I could see other dark shapes moving in the underbrush and hear their rustling all the way back to our tent.

That night I lay awake, thinking of the Anasazi, imagining them here, before they abandoned the mesa to the mule deer, when they would have seen those shapes in the darkness. I thought of the progression from single families living in a hole in the ground to a complex society building a culture, discovering irrigation, ventilation, and architecture virtually on their own, occupying such monuments as the Cliff Palace and Pueblo Bonito and making the complicated social structure to sustain them virtually out of whole cloth. I thought of their disappearance, their moving out and abandoning their culture for reasons as yet uncertain, their blending and merging with the descendants of Hohokam and Mogollon cultures and the nomadic peoples who entered the area long after the Anasazi disappeared. I thought of the long centuries when the Anasazi were lost to time, their buildings crumbling in the canyon crevices and worn away by the winds and rains of the mesa, the brilliant sunlight of the days giving way to inevitable, impenetrable night, the sky ablaze with innumerable stars, all unseen.

The night was without a moon, and the sky was densely packed with stars of every magnitude and configuration. Lying in the tent, staring through the tent flap, dazzled by the shining immensity of the universe, I fell asleep pondering how such a universe would have seemed to a primitive man on a planet blanketed in impenetrable darkness, a man seeing that spectacle through a square window or T-shaped doorway or a kiva smoke hole deep in the recesses of an overhang on the side of a cliff, a man living like a rock dove or a cliff swallow and believing that he and his kind are newcomers to the light, having recently emerged through the Great Sipapu from the underworld.

The ghosts of the Anasazi traveled with us when we left Mesa Verde the next day. They haunted the whole of the Four Corners Area, the canyons and mesas and deserts and mountains. We looked for them in Chaco Canyon, lurching over washboard dirt roads past Navajo hogans to get there, and found them in the sprawling ruins of Pueblo Bonito and the neighboring ruins of Casa Chiquita and Kin Kletso. They were in the straight footpaths across the desert and up the canyon walls to carefully positioned towers and to other ruined villages and family dwellings; they were in the large pueblo of Chetro Ketl farther down Chaco Wash and, across from it, in the elaborate kiva at Casa Rinconada, looking in its restored but still roofless state like a primitive gladiatorial arena; they were in the petroglyphs above Una Vida.

Even after we left Chaco, turning our attention away from archaeology, we still found ourselves among the ghosts of the Southwest, ever among the vanished. At Arches National park vanished rivers had left the eroded shapes that included Sipapu Arch; in the Guadalupe Mountains a vanished sea had left the coral reefs of El Capitan, the fossil-littered floor of McKittrick Canyon, the limestone recesses of Carlsbad Caverns; in Taos and Santa Fe we walked among buildings indebted to Pueblo Indians and Spanish missionaries—in Santa Fe's central marketplace, at a festival of Indian artists, Sue bought a poster of corn kachinas, and later, in Taos, I bought one of La Noche de Zozobra, both celebrations of past rituals. On our night in Santa Fe we took in a movie about the near past and clannish young men who used a Baltimore diner for a kind of communal kiva.

In Bandelier National Monument we hiked through Frijole Canyon, passing the basalt flows and rhyolite tuff tent rocks that gave evidence to the vanished volcanoes nearby. It was our last day in the Southwest. I left our campsite to take a trail across the desert that would bring me out above Frijole Canyon. I watched my footing most of the way, in part because the trail crossed rugged outcroppings of rock close to the canyon rim, in part because I wanted to obey federal warning signs and not "molest" any rattlesnakes, especially inadvertently. Suddenly I was at the edge of the mesa, and I could see the tent rocks in the distance. But unexpectedly, I found myself looking down on Tyuoni Pueblo, Anasazi ruins laid out below me like a stone diagram on the floor of Frijoles Canyon. Nothing was left of the pueblo but the base of its walls, drying in the sun after a brief afternoon rain. In a thicket nearby I could see mule deer moving cautiously, peering out across the empty canyon floor.

In the ways we talk about cultural heritage the Anasazi may matter very little. They seem to be all but untraceable in the modern Pueblo cultures, had no impact on the European heritage that dominates modern American culture, can have no role in the changes a nonwhite, non-European world will make in the cultures of the twenty-first century. And yet they matter still, perhaps because of the changes to come.

We are all Anasazi, always in transition, either in ascent or decline, changing in our agriculture and architecture and art, adding intricacy to our ceremonies and our society, making our inauspicious debut before the footlights of history or mingling undetected among a new troupe of players for a final crowd scene. Our cultures are only kinds of mud wattle, varieties of adobe or stones and mortar, ever in need of repair, restoration, replacement. Culture doesn't solidify like cooled magma; it is always fluid, metamorphic, protean, and even the hardest rock eventually wears away.

In America we like to see ourselves as forever young, a mere two hundred years old and still growing up; we like to think that the destiny of the planet is indistinguishable from our own national future. But the "American Century" is ending, and it will be the only one we get. To our amazement and chagrin all history was not simply a prologue to the American moment, and the past was not only a European past. Here on our own continent others came before us— Hohokam, Mogollon, Hopewell, Anasazi, and countless others— cliff dwellers and mound builders just like us, if on a different scale. Like them, we too are caught in the flow of history—in our turn we are becoming prologue.

Our history is one of deserted dwellings, places recording the different ways we shut off our view of the universe in the recesses of caves and cliffs, pueblos and tenements. The electric canopies that shroud our cities in gray haze hide from us the brilliance and immensity of the night sky, the oldest, most awesome memory of our kind, but we are all Anasazi, newly emergent—once again—from the Great Sipapu, fresh from the underworld of our past lives, fugitives from its ruins.

Knowing Where You've Been
(The Bitterroot Mountains, Montana)

The first afternoon. We head for the Blodgett Creek Trail. Our environmental writing workshop at the Teller Refuge takes up the mornings but leaves us the afternoons free, and the three of us are eager to get out into the Montana wilderness. We are midwestern flatlanders, all raised not far inland from the shores of the Great Lakes, though Ron has been a Montanan for nine years now. Waiting after lunch for someone who never shows up, we start out an hour later than we hoped. I drive the Refuge minivan, and Linda navigates, directing me from Corvallis across the valley floor to Hamilton and into the foothills of the Bitterroot Mountains. Dirt roads take us gradually up out of pastureland into steep forest. We round a bend, cross Blodgett Creek, and park at the trailhead.

Blodgett Creek is swollen and foaming, a roar and blur of tumbling white water just beyond the trees along the trail. In mid-May western Montana is just beginning its second week of summerlike temperatures, and rapid snowmelt generates swift, turbulent runoff. Farmers and ranchers in the Bitterroot Valley worry whether the supply of water will last the growing season.

We strangers, however, eagerly immerse ourselves in new terrain. We set off briskly from the trailhead and, in very little time, see canyon walls, sheer granite facing with jagged rims, emerge above the trees. The trail roughly parallels the creek, passing through narrow bands of ponderosa pine and larch that line its banks. Here the forest is hemmed in by the canyon's narrowness, its inhospitable granite walls, and thick layers of talus piled on the sides of the canyon floor. At a couple of places on the trail we skirt the limits of talus, looking up a forty-five-degree angle across a vast slope of dark boulders that ends a third of the way up toward a sheer precipice. The canyon wall here is so solid and impervious that a channel-less white stream of snowmelt merely slides down the stone face like hose water down a sidewalk.

We dawdle along the trail. Linda identifies the birds, Ron the flowers, trees, and shrubs; I can only nod appreciatively at each of their pronouncements, finding no rhetorical forms to point out in return. We stroll rather than hike, looking around us as we move. We pause to search for a winter wren or a varied thrush singing in the trees, to examine a ring of blue clematis or some alum root saxifrage rising from the mossy ground, to gaze at a bend in the creek where the overflow has created a calm backwater and the dark shape of a trout drifts through dapples of sunlight. At times we dance up the trail, straddling runoff, leaping from stone to stone, dry spot to damp spot, following the worn path of horses and hikers.

An hour into the walk conversation ebbs, and we begin to hike more rapidly. The canyon floor widens, and the trail veers away from the creek bed, still tracing the talus wall. Where the forest opens temporarily at a recent burn, Linda drops behind to write in her journal and return more slowly down the slope; Ron and I quicken our pace through the charred trees and flourishing ground cover. The rocky terrain demands more of our attention as we move. Ahead of us, some three miles up from the trailhead, a pack bridge crosses the creek, and we set that milestone as our destination. We hike with uncertain urgency, knowing that soon we will have to start back to the workshop for evening events.

Sunday hikers coming down the trail greet us. We overtake a slow-moving family who tell us they have seen a moose three hundred yards back, close to the trail. The pack bridge is still perhaps half a mile ahead, but we turn back, searching the brush for the moose we had overlooked in our rush upward. When we find her, she is lying down behind a log, her long dark head raised just into our view, her large ears scanning the sounds around her. The trail is still on

Knowing Where You've Been

rocky ground, but the moose is twenty yards away amid a floor of rich green grass spreading among widely spaced Douglas firs from the slope to the creek. For a few minutes we stand silently, watching her ostentatiously ignore us. Turning back to find her has inadvertently been decisive. By unspoken agreement we hurry back down the trail.

Returning toward the trailhead, I see only the forest ahead of me and occasionally the craggy rim of the canyon emerging on either side. Soon we are in the trees again. I wonder how close we came to the pack bridge, what we might have seen of Blodgett Canyon as we looked back at the Bitterroot Valley crossing the creek, and I find my appetite for the mountains sharpened, not sated, by the hike.

"When you look back at where you have been," Norman Maclean writes, "it often seems as if you have never been there or even as if there were no such place." In his story "USFS 1919: The Logger, the Cook, and the Hole in the Sky" the narrator has paused at the top of a divide, reflecting on where he has been and where he is going. Where he has been is Idaho, at a U.S. Forest Service camp, and more particularly at a lookout tower on Grave Peak; where he is going is Hamilton, in Montana, on the other side of the Bitterroot Mountains, his summer job ended. The distance is thirty-four miles, "fourteen miles up and fourteen miles down with five or six miles still left to go." He intends to walk it in a single day.

Beginning in a mountain meadow he climbs toward gray cliffs that eventually will place him higher than the mountain goats he spots in the distance; along the way he spooks a bull moose on the trail. On the divide, after marking his own version of the state line in urine, he locates Grave Peak. "From the divide the mountain I had lived on was bronze sculpture. It was all shape with nothing on it, just nothing. It was just color and shape and sky." He muses, "So perhaps at a certain perspective what we leave behind is often wonderland, always different from what it was and generally more beautiful."

From the top of the divide, looking into Blodgett Canyon, he recognizes its glacial origins. "Coming at me from almost straight below was a Jacob's ladder of switchbacks, rising out of what I later discovered geologists call a cirque but what to me looked like the original nest of a green coiled glacier." He plunges down the Montana side of the divide, cutting straight across the switchbacks, little avalanches following his path. From the bottom of the basin he follows Blodgett Creek to the mouth of the canyon and trudges the remaining five or six miles to Hamilton.

When I told a friend from Montana that I would be spending a week in the Bitterroot Valley, he referred me immediately to Maclean's story and urged me to hike in the canyon. On the flight west I read the story. Disappointed in its lack of detail about the canyon (it really isn't a hiking story, after all) and immediately aware that I wouldn't have time to trek the fourteen miles to Blodgett Pass, I nonetheless checked the trail in a Bitterroots guide and, before the plane had reached Montanan airspace, set myself that goal of reaching the pack bridge.

Now, as I came away from the canyon, pleased with my companions and energized by the experience of the trail, I realized that I was disappointed, and I struggled to figure out why. Perhaps it had to do with not reaching the pack bridge—with failing to achieve a relatively simple destination—but I wasn't certain why that mattered. Perhaps I hoped to have looked around me and somehow recognized the canyon, discovered the distant switchbacks and the rim of the pass. Perhaps I had hoped that standing on the pack bridge would have placed me so I could see where I had been, where I could be going. While Linda and Ron talked in the van, I tried to remember the words to the children's song about the bear going over the mountain, "to see what he could see." I identified with that bear. As far as I had gone, I still hadn't come away with a sense of knowing where I had been.

The second afternoon. We mill around after the morning workshop, plans shifting, destinations uncertain, finally resolving to go back into the mountains, to another trail. Though eight of us are going, we are all "environmental writers" (by official designation of the institute) and tend to go to wilderness for solitude, not companionship. At the trailhead people plan to drop out or stay behind, and the progress up the Mill Creek Trail spreads us out and separates us. Some start out slowly and fall to the rear; others keep on far enough to separate themselves from those behind, then slow down to let those ahead go on without them.

Mill Creek is only a few miles north of Blodgett Creek, descending at the easternmost point of the promontory between Blodgett Canyon and the next canyon north. After a short stretch in open forest, the terrain is often rocky. The forest is dense and broad on either side of the stream, unrestrained by canyon walls. A mile or so along the trail we cross to the north side of the creek on a solid double-log bridge and find ourselves moving parallel to the creek but often away from its banks, intermittently but persistently climbing. Not far beyond the bridge the group is reduced to Ron, Jeff, and me. We begin to push ourselves to reach the falls a couple more miles ahead, making it harder on ourselves by talking about writing most of the way without slackening our pace.

For a little while we parallel sheer canyon walls, but soon we are deep into the forest. The walking is easier than in Blodgett Canyon, the terrain more varied, the forest seemingly older, denser. Within a couple miles of the log bridge, past a large boulder and a big wooden sign, we enter the Selway-Bitterroot National Wilderness. Soon the trail steepens and repeatedly winds away from the creek until a final loop brings it closer again. The creek's continuous rumble becomes a roar. Through the trees we can see the foaming waters of the falls and follow the trail up to an opening in the forest near the top.

Beyond the clearing the ground rises sharply again, and ahead of us the trail disappears back into forest, but this rounded hump of basalt is covered shallowly with only lichens, wildflowers, and low grasses. Near the creek nothing grows except for a few stunted pines; most of the rock is naked and exposed, shaved clean by plummeting snowmelt. Upstream the forest closes in tightly on the creek bed; below the falls the creek is all foamy billows of whitewater slicing through towering forests of ponderosa pine and Douglas fir; across the stream, on the south bank, the trees are thick, impenetrable. Only on the north bank of the falls is the rock swept clean and the surface open to the sun.

We take our time surveying the falls, moving slowly up and down its rock face to consider it from above and below, all the while inundated by the sound of mountain water. As falls go, this one is neither majestic nor exceptional, angling down sixty to eighty feet or so rather than plunging vertically from the lip of a precipice. Swollen with snowmelt, its foam as white as the snowpack that feeds it, the creek plummets over rugged terraces and outcroppings. We feel its wild power and stand smiling in the spray and the sound, respectful of its reckless turbulence.

The roar makes conversation difficult, but Jeff and Ron survey the plant life away from the brink, and we each independently declare a desire to camp on the level ground across the clearing. Someone wonders where the trail goes, and I look longingly at the point where it reenters the forest and disappears. The wall of trees prevents us from knowing where we might have gone, and, aware that we have overstayed, we turn back toward where we have been to head down the mountainside toward the trailhead and the rest of our party. Our retreat is so swift that I don't notice when I can no longer hear the thunder of the falls, and our pace allows me no time to look back.

When I asked my friend from Montana about places to hike in the Bitterroot Valley, he looked thoughtful for a moment, shook his head, and said, "Well, as early as you're going, there'll be too much snow to bag a peak." I laughed and assured him that "bagging a peak" wasn't a priority with me. But the term tended to stay with me on the trip, especially as I trudged along the flat farm roads of the Teller Refuge where the snow-capped peaks of the Bitterroot Range punctuated the horizon. After our return from the Mill Creek Trail, when someone asked me later in the day if I had been "one of the *men* who

Knowing Where You've Been

had gone for distance" on the trail, I thought again about the concept of bagging a peak.

We'd come back to the Mill Creek Trailhead to find the van gone and a note promising that someone would return for us. No doubt we'd delayed people eager to get back to the Refuge, and those who'd stopped along the way had returned to the trailhead with a sense of accomplishment and completion far sooner than we had. If they had been waiting for us, we owed them apologies. But I really couldn't accept the implicit gender explanation for our approach to the hike—after all, I knew from reading their essays that some of the women in the Environmental Writing Institute had had far more arduous adventures than I was ever likely to attempt. The only peaks I've "bagged" not only have *not* been hard to reach but also were ascended for the view rather than for distance or height.

But the Mill Creek Falls hadn't been a peak, after all, and its distance had only been a few miles. Though I knew what *hadn't* moved me to reach the falls, I wasn't certain what *had* or why it felt so good to have been there.

The final afternoon. The morning workshop over, the group disperses for various tours and activities. Ron, Valerie, and I meet Janine Benyus and her father, Doug, who both live in the Bitterroot Valley. Janine, whose *Northwoods Wildlife Guide* I value, has volunteered to take workshoppers hiking. Somehow I expect a leisurely excursion and don't bother to change out of sneakers. Although her plan had been to take us to either Blodgett or Mill Creek, when she learns that Ron and I have been to both, she opts for the Bear Creek Overlook Trail instead, a change from creek bed habitat, a promise of a vista.

Janine drives the minivan to the trailhead, pointing out from the highway the shoulder of the mountain where the Bear Creek Overlook is located. We climb the foothills on back roads threading through pasturelands then swing onto a twisting, narrow, shoulderless dirt road, an eighty-degree grade sloping away from it. In the front passenger seat my attention is divided between Janine's conversation and the slope we lean toward with every other lurch of the vehicle. Doug Benyus recounts hitting a patch of ice on otherwise dry road a few weeks earlier and plunging over the edge in a Toyota Four-Runner; luckily, he had hit a tree a little ways past the edge and was able to back up the slope and continue down the road. Father and daughter tell of other switchback terrors as we ride, but Janine doesn't slow down. I tell myself she knows how to drive these roads better than I, and remind myself to sit in the back on the way down.

The trailhead is an open area on the side of the mountain, with the valley floor a couple thousand feet below, spread out in a gray haze not thick enough to obscure the distant outline of the Sapphire Mountains across the valley. We set out hiking easily through open forest. Lodgepole pines tower above us; the forest floor is carpeted with needles. The wide trail follows a series of switchbacks that take us rapidly up the mountainside with little need for the attentive footing that the creek trails demanded. The day is warm, the mountain breezes refreshing, and our progress consistent. We pause from time to time when Janine draws our attention to some element of the habitat—dwarf mistletoe sprouting from a limb of lodgepole pine, its seeds released by an inner "spring" that fires it fifty feet into the forest, to stick to another tree or be transported on the feathers of the bird that triggered its release; the activity of pitch beetles that bore into pines and, through a symbiotic relationship with bacteria in their mouths and their own excavating, girdle a tree and plug its channels of sap until the tree dies; a blue grouse spooked by Doug Benyus's hound, Barney, fluttering out of reach into a spruce and perching, immobile, waiting for us to lose sight of her. The Benyuses instruct us through a genial symbiosis, feeding each other questions, volunteering each other's information.

Less than halfway up the trail we discover patches of snow across the path. The trees change to spruce and Douglas fir. We look for blazed tree trunks more frequently now, as the trail disappears beneath the snow for longer and longer stretches. Finally, an hour or so into the trail, we reach a turn of a switchback and see an unbroken

Knowing Where You've Been

field of snow stretching through the trees. Janine tells us that it will be mostly snow the rest of the way and gives us the option of struggling up the slope or turning back and looking for a creek bed. Valerie votes for turning back. Ron and I make noises about not caring either way until the possibility of turning back becomes too real; then we admit to wanting to continue to the overlook. We have seen creek beds, we say, and Valerie urges us to go on, while she meanders back.

We are all in T-shirts, Janine and Ron in shorts, but are kept warm by exertion as we cross the snow. We slip with every step as it gives way beneath us. Often we find ourselves postholing across the snow, sinking in past our ankles, sometimes up to our knees. On separate occasions Janine and I each strike a pocket of air beneath the snow, where it has covered a fallen tree, and plunge in up to our crotches with one leg while the other slips across firmer footing. The icy granules of snow soak through my sneakers and socks, and I grumble to myself about my lack of planning until I realize that my hiking boots too would have eventually succumbed to wetness.

It takes us longer than we hoped to reach the crest. The terrain opens up, the trees more stunted and sparse than at lower levels, the snow ranging in ever larger fields. Suddenly we emerge onto the base of a rocky ridge. The timbers of a collapsed line cabin or watchtower poke through a deep covering of empacked snow. Rising above the ridge is a barren crag with contorted shapes of scrub around its base; through the trees on the top of the ridge I look across at a snowy peak dotted with scruffy trees, extending another thousand feet or more above us. The way to the top of the crag is rough and tricky, along precipices and across barren, lichen-free basalt. The west side of our mountain is almost vertical, nearly devoid of plant life except for occasional pioneers jutting from scanty toeholds in the cliff face. But from that exposed peninsula of rock the three valleys of Bear Creek open out to us.

Directly to the west the South Fork of Bear Creek runs down the center of the valley, lush and green and thickly carpeted with conifers. From where we stand, we can see the mountains beyond the valley, the distant sources of Bear Creek's water. To the northwest is another valley, another fork of the creek, that we can trace glinting through the trees until it divides into two more streams, the Middle and North Forks, each descending its own valley. The trees thin out along the slopes of these valleys, turn darker the higher up they go, until they are only random silhouettes against ever-broadening snowfields. All the peaks around us are snow covered, as must be the peak of the mountain upon whose shoulder we stand.

We are viewing classic glacial terrain. Empty white basins of snow identify cirques, the glacial bowls that will become Bryan Lake and Bear Lake by the end of summer. Above and around them are weathered horns and arêtes, the peaks that formed them and the ridges that hold them in place; the valleys extending from the cirques take the wide U-shape of the glaciers that carved them. Directly below us the merged forks of Bear Creek produce a wide foaming cataract rushing snowmelt and glacial debris toward the outwash plains that form part of the foothills.

Janine tells us that when the Pacific plate pushed under the North American plate, it raised the mountains of the Idaho Batholith to a point where the mountaintops became unstable and slid off to the east, creating the broad level plain that would become the Bitterroot Valley (itself later scoured by glaciers) and ending up as the Sapphire Mountains. From this crag we can see beyond the Sapphires to spires of the Garnet Range and the Continental Divide near Anaconda. We can also see a long way toward the beginning of time.

I slowly scan it all with my binoculars. I know that I could sit for hours minutely surveying those valleys and still not feel I had taken them in. Nonetheless, I feel myself smiling all the while, feel myself stirred and moved by everything around me. It isn't just the beauty, though it is transcendently beautiful, and it certainly isn't the distance, because everything around us reminds us of how much farther we could go. It isn't how far at all but how deep.

That's it. That's the epiphany that dispels my uncertainty about my motives on these hikes. That's what I've been pursuing after all.

I simply need to go as deeply into wilderness as it takes before the wilderness comes into me. Sometimes you need to go as deeply as possible where you've never been to reach a place you recognize at once, recognize entirely. That's where I find myself in the Bitterroots.

We stand there a while longer, reveling in arrival. When we finally, reluctantly, turn to descend, I don't need to look back to know where I've been.

four

Shore Lines
(The Great Lakes)

1. Inland

I have mostly lived an inland life, measuring out my youth in rural New York towns, my adulthood among the farmlands of Iowa and the middle of Michigan's Lower Peninsula. Lockport, the city of my childhood, was about fifteen miles south of Lake Ontario. From certain points along the ridge on the top of the Niagara Escarpment, it was possible on clear days to see the lake beyond the flat lake plain, a promise of a promise. But Lockport itself was a landlocked city, a port on the Erie Barge Canal, its locks constructed to allow canal freight to ascend or descend the escarpment. We lived in the south end of the city, beyond yet another ridge.

To make a day trip to Lake Ontario, as we did so often in the summers of the late 1940s and early 1950s, we drove up to High Street, on the top of the ridge, then made a series of descents to the lake plain. Most of the way the roads to Olcott and its beaches and amusement parks were crowded with traffic converging on the shoreline. My grandfather usually drove us, cautiously taking us down the same roads we sometimes took on occasional visits to elderly relatives in country houses where my grandparents had grown up. The crowded family car, the towns, the familiar roads to family farmsteads, the long stretches of fields and orchards, all combined to give me a certain inland feeling, even though I knew our destination.

Yet somewhere, maybe on the rise just before the final slope descending into Olcott, the air changed, grew lighter, clearer, moist, with a different scent and taste than the humid air of cornfields and orchards. Almost at once the houses changed, the landed, farmstead look giving way to lake-aspiring resort architecture. Even before I spotted the taffy shack on the outskirts of Olcott, I felt myself in the presence of the lake, no longer an inland creature but a shoreline pilgrim nearing my destination. And then we topped the rise and barely glimpsed the lake in the distance before losing sight of it again, but the single glimpse kept me looking for it, alive to its nearness and to an imminent sense of arrival.

In those days tiny cottages were wedged together in worn clusters close along the beachfront, surrounded by narrow yards barely large enough for the fences people put on them. Sometimes they washed out in the high tides of storms or stayed surrounded by shallow pools of water well into summer. The streets around the beach were lined with bars, restaurants, arcades, amusement parks, and souvenir shops. Olcott was a resort town, comatose in the winter, hyperactive in summer.

Sometimes Grandpa let the women and children out of the car near the beach, but most often we turned onto the main street and cruised slowly through the clamor of dodge-'em cars, Ferris wheels, and carousels, the lights and music and dull chatter of thronging idlers and midway games, the mysterious depths of arcades darkened in the glare of the sun. We parked in a distant area crowded with other cars then carried blankets, bags, and baskets through open, grassy picnic areas shaded by tall trees and dotted with charcoal grills and picnic tables, until we looked down on the lake.

To reach the principal public beach we descended concrete stairs that passed through terraced lawn bounded by high stone walls. The actual beach itself was a narrow strip of sand, easy prey to erosion against the breakwall that held up the lowest section of the lawn. A long concrete pier shaped like an upside-down, backward-ʟ stretched out into Lake Ontario, a further hedge against erosion. During our years there it had already begun a slow-motion collapse under the battering of lake storms. On every trip to Olcott we walked out to the end of it, where the fishermen were; often my grandfather took a fishing pole and tackle box out to the end and spent the day apart from the women and children, talking and drinking with the other fishermen.

But the end of the pier was a long walk on bare feet across flat concrete grilling in the summer sun, and the sections that were disintegrating were rough and jagged and tilted toward the water. Kids were discouraged from going out, and the surly old men fishing at the end reinforced the exclusion. I was seldom tempted beyond the shoreline. The end of the pier only made me feel more isolated, separated from both land and lake on a skinny, artificial extension of beach.

The swimming area was close to the shore and always crowded, like the thickly blanketed stretch of beach. We jumped into the lake off the pier only where the water never came over our heads. Sometimes we went on the west side of the pier, away from the official beach protected by the angle of the l, to let ourselves be caught and buffeted by stronger waves that never made it into the beach area. I never stayed in the water very long and among the traffic of the beach found little room to play in the sand.

. My days in Olcott were overcrowded, dank, and noisy; although I thrilled to that first scent of the Great Lakes in the air, the first sense of the shoreline's imminence, I was excited more by the prospect of hot dog and cotton candy stands, pinball games and penny arcades, than by the beach. It made me restless to sit burning in the sun, and an uncle who had tried the "sink or swim" method of teaching me to swim had me wary of deep waters. I was always eager to get over to the arcades. I especially thrilled to the nickelodeons with their silent cartoons and western movies. I couldn't wait to step up on the footstand, press my face against the eyepiece, and set still pictures into motion with the handle on the side of the machine.

Once, probably by accident, I put my money in the wrong machine and cranked around a showing of *September Morn*. It was a film recreation of the painting, and my first sight of the naked female form. More in surprise than excitement, I watched the nude woman frolicking in a forest pond for a few minutes and wondered when something would happen other than her soundless giggling and splashing. Her nakedness, for me, was insufficient reason to watch the film; I wanted some hint of story. The silence and the jerky motion of the individual frames turning at uneven speed made the scene unreal enough, but I found the lack of narrative frustrating, and her prancing grew tedious even within minutes. As I cranked and watched, I kept glancing at a machine I coveted that played an old western. The moment it became available, I abandoned the nude bather in mid-frolic.

For me coming to the lake was always another opportunity to recreate this moment: my face pressed against the metal sides of the viewing box, the grainy, jerky motion of fist fights and gun fights and chases on horseback flickering silently in front of me, the beeps and dings and thumps and whooshes of pinball machines and target rifles and miniature football games barely noticeable in my concentration. The lake was nowhere in my thoughts, as distant beyond the arcade walls, the crowded streets, the lawns, the concrete, and the stone, as if it had evaporated into Niagara County farmland. This strip of tawdry midway shoreline seemed as broad as all the world.

2. Lake View

I attended an inland college in the 1960s. At Geneseo, when New Yorkers and Long Islanders spoke with casual superiority of "The City" and "The Island," as if there could be only one possible reference point for each, I retaliated with allusions to "The Lake," even though for a Lockport boy references to "The Canal" would have been more appropriate. Perhaps it was simply a matter of scale, the way the city and island dwellers would have been overwhelmed by the scope of Lake Ontario if they comprehended it at all. But perhaps all those childhood visits to the shoreline had made me feel, in spite of my arcade preoccupations, as if something more lay beyond it. Now farther inland, I came to think of myself as someone who dwelt by water, and for a time after college I was.

I taught high school English in Wilson, a quiet Lake Ontario town six miles west of Olcott. By the time I lived there, the shoreline was under siege, the chemical pollution of the Niagara River giving rise to massive fish kills and weedy lake floor growth. The waters of Lake Ontario, always an opaque green, had become murkier still, the texture of a thin pea soup, a churning biochemical gruel. At Olcott the smell of rotting fish and algae and weeds closed the beaches. The pier collapsed into the lake, neglected and unmourned. The very existence of the town itself seemed to shudder on weak pilings. Wilson was less affected by the condition of the lake because it wasn't dependent on day visitors. The whole of its shoreline was hemmed in by homes and summer cottages. Occasional stretches of highway afforded only brief panoramic glimpses of the lake, no place to turn off and ponder the view.

My teaching colleagues and I talked often of sailing, but the only time I actually went out on the lake was in a guidance counselor's cabin cruiser. Four or five of us stood in the back of the boat, sipping beer from the case of bottles at our feet, and tried to bellow conversationally above the roar of the engine. The wind buffeted us, the hull throbbed and shuddered beneath us, the keel punched its way across the waves with regularly spaced jolts that continually tested our balance. This nightmarish, pointless outing only made me more supportive of vicarious sailing. Far better it was to go down to the marina late Friday afternoon for a few beers, the weekly fish fry, and the companionship of colleagues and friends. The Boat House, a marina restaurant, was right beside the boat ramp; its lower story was a tackle shop and boat rental. We always hoped for tables on the porch above the rental dock, with breezes blowing off the lake and sail and powerboats rocking in their slips across the marina.

Wilson essentially had no beach. The marina occupied the only lowland around the harbor. Both east and west of town the shoreline rose quickly, and the beach became a thin margin of stones, boulders, and debris below steep, overgrown bluffs ten to thirty feet high. Walking along the shoreline meant walking along the edge of the bluffs, where most of the frontage was filled with privately owned cottages and year-round homes set far back from the lakeshore road. From both places I lived in Wilson, my walk to the lake crossed a landlord's lawn and ended on a bluff, with no access to the water at all.

One day I ventured off from my apartment in search of walkable shoreline. I crossed an overgrown field of land purchased by the

state for a long-delayed park and descended low bluffs onto a narrow strand of pebbly beach from which grew enormous cottonwoods.
The strand was the only land link to Sunset Island, usually only accessible by boat from the marina. On one side of the strand was Lake
Ontario, on the other a thick marsh, its waters renewed by rain and
rising waves from storms. I crossed the strand, picking my way carefully, and scrambled onto the island.

Sunset Island was private property, a dense cluster of vacation cottages that huddled shoulder to shoulder across the convex surface
of the island, extending to its peripheries. In its heyday, when the
railroad had put in a special spur for its owners, it had been a bustling place. But the close proximity of its buildings, the isolation of
the town, the loss of beach frontage, all had reduced it from its glory
days. Especially now, in the middle of autumn, it seemed weathered,
desolate, forlorn. The island was shaped like a turtle's shell, and the
land rose gradually from the shoreline. Many of the cottages were
two-story houses, and all the buildings were strewn in close clusters across an unending lawn devoid of walkways or paths. Only the
outer fringe of buildings on the north side of the island had a view of
the lake; the rest had views chiefly of the other cottages surrounding
them. Padlocked, shuttered, boarded up for the winter, they gave a
haunted air to the island even in daylight. I walked among the silent
buildings as the sun went down, feeling increasingly chilled in their
shadows, and had to rush across the strand before nightfall stranded
me on the island. The cottages didn't seem to bring me closer to the
lake, only nearer.

Still, in time, it seemed to be enough to know the lake was there, if
only in the distance. I made a habit of monitoring its mood. When I
rose in the morning, my first act was to stumble to the lakeside windows and check the lake, scanning the horizon for distant vessels,
noting whether the lake and the sky were blue or whether the sky was
gray and the lake an opaque green roiling with whitecaps. As often
as I could, I walked out to the bluffs and stood in the wind from the
lake to gaze north. Listening to the waves roll in, I tuned myself to

their rhythm. In winter I chronicled the slow buildup of ice, a growing white stucco landscape moving away from the shore, encroaching on the waters; in spring I watched the progress of the season in the progress of the lake as it melted its way back toward the bluff. Sometimes the lake seemed the measure of my own moods. I came to value my time on the shoreline, even though the bluffs kept me at a distance from the lake. When I moved inland again, I continually felt the absence of the lake in the view from my windows.

3. Shallows

It is the Fourth of July, neighborhood reunion and block party time on Ridgeway Avenue in St. Joseph, Michigan. By midafternoon the morning hubbub—tennis matches and foot races, family street parade and Rousing Speaker, potluck lunch in the Prestons' yard—has given way to quiet. My wife's father and mother grew up on this street and returned to live in one of the family houses. Since the beginning of the 1980s, first as a boyfriend, then as a husband, I have been coming with my wife and children to the house on Ridgeway.

The house is large and airy, one of the original buildings constructed when the north shore area was first developed as a private club near the turn of the century. St. Joseph and its sister city, Benton Harbor, then were resorts and spas with regular rail and steamship service from Chicago. The bedroom windows on the front of the house have a view of Lake Michigan in the distance. Lake-effect snowstorms and rains strike here first; from the upstairs windows we can watch the weather change a long way out on the lake. But each year it grows more difficult to see the beach itself as newer houses intrude themselves into the view.

Where once the houses kept close to the street itself, leaving a buffer zone of beach grass and dunes and an open view of the lake, more recent residents have built sprawling new homes as close to the crest of the foredune as possible, dominating the view and appropriating it for themselves. The older residents maintained a communal attitude toward the stretch of beach running parallel to their street, an attitude developed when the beach was club property, open only to members; newcomers are less communal, more inclined to build borders around their beachfront, if only by attitude. We pass one of the newer homes on our trek to the beach, a house dug out of the dunes with a long blacktop driveway paralleling the path. Where the path rises on the foredune we pass a large, glassed-in, triangular room and the wooden deck that extends from it. The house is shaped like a boat cresting a wave of sand and has become a conspicuous landmark from the lake. Boats and picnic tables and grills and beach umbrellas spill across the dune and down onto the beach, the turf markers of ostentatious consumers.

During Fourth of July afternoons families withdraw to the beach in retreat from the relentless conviviality of the morning. Conversations are quieter, family groups tend to stay closer together, the children play Marco Polo tirelessly, while grownups check up on them in intervals between chatting and dozing. Beyond the sandbar, wherever it has relocated itself over the winter, the surface of the lake is continually crisscrossed with sailboats and cabin cruisers and Jet Skis and water skiers and windsurfers and rubber rafts and dinghies. The people in the boat-shaped house bring their boats close to the shore, where older residents keep a watchful eye on their grandchildren and lament the gas fumes floating on the breeze. In the evening the beach becomes a busy walkway for people on their way to the pier for a fireworks display, threading their way among the beach fires and random bottle rockets being set off along the way. The pier and the beach around it get crowded, and the sparkling bursts of aerial fireworks above the lake set off waves of appreciative "ooohs" and, when volleys of them rocket overhead, delighted cheers.

The bustling activity of the beach on the Fourth is simply an extension of the morning events and troubles no one very much. We have walked this beach in solitude before and know we will again. It is an ideal stretch of shoreline. From the lighthouse pier and the harbor channel that mark its southern limit, the beach, wide and gently sloping, extends north a mile or more to the public park, bounded on the east by a twenty-foot wall of sand topped by beach grass. At the park the beach opens up for greater use, cuts back to a higher ring of dunes. Beyond the park the bluffs rise fifty, eighty, a hundred feet, and trees line the top of the wall of sand into the distance, where the shoreline arches gently around to a point fifteen miles away. White clouds of steam from a nuclear power plant interrupt the thin line of darkness before it disappears. Often, on clear days, a beachcomber can survey the horizon from the pier to the point and not see another person, despite the twin cities just beyond the dunes.

The water is shallow and the bottom sandy a long way out, and usually a tall child or an adult can walk out to a sandbar without having to swim at all. One July evening only my wife's family was on the beach. While everyone else conversed on the sand, I made my way toward the sandbar. The water was cool, but I gradually got used to it and floated and swam in short bursts of energy. When I finally started back toward land, I saw my wife on the verge of the lake, trying to get my attention. She gestured for me to look behind me. I couldn't hear what she was calling, but when I turned around, I realized she had been saying, "Sunset."

The sun had been low and a pale and hazy ochre when we had arrived, but as it set it was growing more vividly orange. The water was calm, the sky cloudless, the sun very low and large. I started moving back out toward the sandbar, lowering myself in the water to paddle in the sun's reflection. The sun seemed to enlarge itself, turn scarlet then crimson. The sky became a vivid color wheel. The lake grew calmer, more placid, as if adjusting itself to more fully catch the sun's reflection. I waited, spellbound, as the sun touched the lake and began slowly to disappear into it. As more of the sun set beyond the horizon, more of its rays diffused themselves across the water. For those moments the world was only sun and sky and water; the world was reduced to its essentials, and I, kneeling in the water on the sandbar, was somehow alone in the center of its mystery. The sun yawned on the horizon, opening like a glowing red doorway, rolling a gently undulating pathway toward me. If I could move quickly enough, before it dropped much lower, I could go inside, pass through that portal. But I was transfixed, suspended; I could only watch it sink deeper into Lake Michigan.

As the sun set, the air grew cooler, and I began to feel chilled. My wife was gathering up her towel and waving me in; the others had already moved toward the path up across the dunes. I waded in, dried myself, and followed them. At the top of the foredune twilight blazed across the windows of the ship-shaped house, but the room and the deck before it were empty. I looked back at the sun, two-thirds of it set and a gray haze spreading across the dull red of what remained, and felt a curious longing, a sense of having left unsatisfied.

As I trudged across the darkening dunes, it seemed to me that I am too often satisfied by being on the shoreline, certain of the world to the limits of my vision, within the narrow circumference of my encircling horizons. I wondered whether I take too much comfort in its limits, too easily accept that the journey ends at the threshold and not in the spaces beyond it. That night when I shut my eyes in bed, my vision filled with red. I fell asleep remembering myself in the water, alone with the sunset.

4. Immersion

A few miles before the road to the tip of the Leelanau Peninsula ends at Lighthouse Point, a side road leads off to an isolated section of the state park crisscrossed with hiking trails. One trail goes along the marshy shore of Mud Lake, others circle through interior ridges of forest, and one leads out to Cathead Bay. A wide strip of sand spreads from the waters, scooped and smoothed from a range of low parallel dunes dotted with wildflowers and beach grass, beyond which a forest rises on the heights, oak and arbor vitae giving way farther inland to birch and maple and pine.

I came there for the first time one sweltering summer day, fleeing the crowded, cranky tourism of Traverse City and a heavy schedule of responsibilities. I followed the rough, dusty road in from the highway, spooking a pair of young deer as I rounded a curve, and found myself parking in a spacious but deserted dirt lot. Giving only a cursory glance at the large wooden trail map, I struck off down the nearest trail. Eventually, I found myself climbing a wooden set of stairs toward the top of a sandy, tree-lined ridge and a squat wooden platform.

On three sides low shrubs and burr oak closed the Manitou Overlook off from any view back into the forest, but the fourth side was open and overlooked the bay. In the far distance, across Lake Michigan, I could see the Fox Islands, two hazy humps rising from the water. Near the platform the ridge fell away sharply down to a low bowl of sand with an island of juniper bushes in the center; beyond the bowl hillocks and gullies of sand stretched out toward the lake.

The day was shimmeringly hot and the lake a cool, placid blue. Sweat trickled down my face and stung my eyes, and a breeze from the lake brought with it a slight hint of coolness. In an instant I decided to leave my daypack on the platform, vault the railing, and strike out toward the shoreline. I dropped off the platform, took long, rapid strides down the steep sand hill, then trudged more slowly across the dunes. When I reached the foredune, it rose slightly ahead of me, making my first sight of the beach a moment of surprise and drama. For a moment I stood there, gazing at the broad arch of sand, cooling in a light breeze, and then slid down the embankment. I crossed the beach until I was a few feet from the waves and then rotated slowly, taking in the encircling wall of dune, the beach curving in either direction to the limits of my vision, the seemingly limitless lake merging with the sky. I heard the wind rushing past my ears, the waves uncurling at my feet, the slightest whisper of blowing sand behind me. Serenity seemed to settle on me like a mist.

And I was the only one on the beach. The dunes hid the platform from me and I from it, and I felt entirely alone in the whole expanse of park. I opened my shirt to the breeze, kicked off my shoes, peeled off my socks to welcome the waves across my feet. I closed my eyes and lifted my face toward the sky. I was aware only of sensation tingling through, and as I welcomed it, I began to strip off the rest of my clothing. I moved out into waves, letting the thrilling coolness of the water slowly rise up my body. Pausing every so often to let waves rush past me, I felt like a living sequel to *September Morn*. I dove beneath the surface, the sudden shock instantaneously dissipating into thrill. All the elements—sun, lake, wind—made all my senses more acute. I swam and paddled and dove and dug my toes into the sandy bottom, reveling in sensation. Then I stood still in the water, submerged to my chin, my eyes closed against the sun's glare, face lifted into the breeze, and time evaporated. Soon I felt myself disengaging, drifting out of the world, as if I'd been given permission to shed my temporal existence with my clothing, as if I could rinse away particles of cognition and memory like specks of beach sand.

And yet, even in an interlude of disintegrating self, I felt somehow more connected, as if I had finally arrived. There are times when you feel for once that you are not your mind but your senses. There are times when you have to receive the world without mediation, without the bending of light in the prisms of self and species and society. In such times you begin at the shorelines, embraced by sun and lake, and spiral outward from your shrinking self, toward infinity.

Time passed without appearing to pass. I opened my eyes and let the world slowly slip back into me. I rose up in the shallows and waded out of the lake. As I crossed the beach toward the driftwood log where I had left my clothing, I caught a movement in the distance and saw two tiny figures emerge from the dunes along the beach to the south, where the trail must be. I looked back at the lake, gathered up my clothes, and, still naked and dripping, headed back into the dunes to find a place to let sun and wind dry me. It didn't take long to feel the sun's sticky heat again, but I didn't mind. I'd crossed the threshold, gone far enough beyond the boundary. The shoreline no longer felt like a limit. Rather, it seemed to me a promise fulfilled.

Of Trees and Time
(Warren Woods, Michigan)

It is not only the size of the trees. It is the assembly of species. The stark rise of their trunks against the sky. . . . It is the long line of sight, the open aspect afforded by the lack of any significant shrub layer. It is the sad rarity of strands with the integrity of this one.

—LAURIE ALLMAN ON WARREN WOODS in *Far from Tame: Reflections from the Heart of a Continent*

We came to Warren Woods from St. Joseph, about twenty miles north, on the Lake Michigan shoreline. The previous day we had joined Sue's family for a Fourth of July block party on the street where her grandparents had first built their homes and where she and her parents and her siblings had grown up. Some houses were owned by the third generation of a family, fourth and fifth generations attended the party, but many of the old houses and a number of huge, aggressively positioned new houses were owned by strangers to the street or transplants to the town. I'd been coming to the party for an even twenty years and in the beginning had been beguiled by the continuity of the community, the lineage revealed in resemblances, the air of permanence about the place. But lately we had begun to feel dislocated, on unfamiliar terrain. My father-in-law had died two years earlier, on his favorite holiday, the Fourth of July; with each passing year we saw fewer of his generation, and fewer faces in the crowd belonged to direct descendants of the street's original inhabitants. Our own daughters, who had been children when they began coming, were independent adults as they returned this year, and one of them brought a new husband with her. We were constantly aware of how much succeeding generations were filling the spaces opened up by the passing of the generations before.

So, when we turned south toward Warren Woods instead of north toward home, postponing for another day a return to the routine of our lives, we were hoping in part to find a way to step out of the flow of time, so heavy on our minds. My wife had grown up in Berrien County, but she had never been to Warren Woods Natural Area and was as unfamiliar with the rolling farmlands around it as I was. We had been to Warren Dunes State Park, the other great legacy of Edward K. Warren, who'd bought up the dunes along the lake after he'd already purchased two hundred acres of woods in the center of prime farmland; in 1879 he'd already been aware, even in the heady, profit-driven development frenzy of the late nineteenth century, that something needed to be set aside from all the clearing, plowing, and logging that was transforming the southwestern corner of Michigan. Because of Warren's foresight at the end of the nineteenth century, we would be able to walk at the beginning of the twenty-first century through forest that had never been logged.

We went to the southern main entrance of the woods first. Passing through open fields on a dirt road, we entered the shade of the forest and saw at once a doe and two fawns in the road. I stopped the car, and we waited for them to move. In their blank expressions I read surprise and curiosity, like a rural family wondering about unexpected visitors from town. With unhurried grace the doe bounded into the woods, and the fawns quickly followed, and we passed the place where they had vanished slowly, pleased to have been greeted at the threshold of the preserve.

I had known that the suspension bridge across the Galien River, which had given access to the most extensive portion of Warren Woods, had been swept away by flooding in 1996, but I hadn't checked to see if it had been restored. In the parking lot off the southern entrance, the indication that guiding signs had been removed suggested that it hadn't been replaced, so we returned to the car and went out into

Of Trees and Time

the farmland again to circle around to the northern entrance, where we parked on the shoulder of the road.

Almost at once we knew we had entered someplace special. Attracted by the loud whistling of a nearby bird, we tracked down the singer, a hooded warbler, his face and forehead and breast bright golden, a black cowl or hood completely encircling his face. Neither of us had encountered a hooded warbler before, and here he was, almost insistent upon introducing himself to us.

"This is the forest primeval." The phrase from Longfellow's *Evangeline* helped motivate Warren's preservation. The woods had only been partly logged when Warren purchased them, and he was aware of how quickly the primeval forests were vanishing. Except for the circle trail looping around a bend of the Galien River and the trails that connect the loop to the north and south ends of the preserve, nothing has been done to manage or develop the natural area. This is beech-maple climax forest, about as extensive a stand of "virgin" forest as can be found in the Lower Peninsula of Michigan. More majestic in scale even than the Valley of the Giants stand of cedars on South Manitou Island or the white pines of Hartwick Pines State Park or the Estivant Pines Nature Sanctuary on the Keweenaw Peninsula, in Michigan Warren Woods can be only be surpassed by the remote fastnesses of the Porcupine Mountains. But all of those are northwoods forests; this is the last remnant of the forest that covered the southern portion of the state. The hardest thing to get your mind around, once you've trod into the center of the natural area, is the realization that all that farmland, all that open space you drove through to get here, once was filled with forest just like this. In Warren Woods trees can grow over 125 feet tall, be more than 5 feet in diameter, have lived for more than four centuries.

Soon after we entered the woods from the northern boundary, we stopped before a tremendous beech, hollowed at its base, standing like a giant on tiptoes. A little farther on we approached an enormous maple, its leaves so high above the forest floor that I needed binoculars to see them clearly in the morning sun. We moved slowly down the trail, pausing at another and yet another tree of gigantic dimensions. Although we are frequent wanderers of the forests throughout the state, we were unprepared for trees of these proportions, particularly in such plenty. The undergrowth on the forest floor consisted mostly of the prodigy of the giant trees, waiting their turn in forest succession; a stand of young maple saplings filled a rare open area of sunlight, and in much of the forest the shade of the canopy and the thick litter of fallen leaves kept the ground open. One huge fallen beech lay across the trail, broken at base but still attached to the stump, its trunk split and sundered, exposing the musculature inside. We could easily walk underneath it, but had it separated from the stump entirely, we would have been challenged to clamber over it.

The trail into the loop from the north boundary crossed high ground, and eventually we descended easily from the bluffs down to the floodplain of the meandering Galien River. We'd come too late in the season to catch the wildflowers that blossom before the leafy canopy closes off the sunlight, but in a marshy clearing my wife pointed out a Michigan lily (also called the Turk's-cap lily) gleaming alone, yellow-orange, in the sun. In nearby sycamores a yellow-throated warbler momentarily danced in and out of view before leaving us alone on the riverbank. The path led to the foundations of the suspension bridge, and we saw its broken remnants on the other side of the river. Upstream, two deadfalls formed natural bridges, but we were content to stay on the northern bank and followed the path farther along the river. The Galien was thick, chicken gravy–brown, and slow.

Not far from the riverbank a sycamore grew with a double trunk, one at a sharp angle above the ground and the other curving away as if it longed to go straight to the sky. A slender straight horse chestnut grew alongside the sycamore, and farther down we came upon a rock elm. We looked around for more of the variety of trees we knew to be in the floodplain—tulip tree, white ash, red maple, basswood, butternut. The trail led back around to the bluff, a steeper climb at this point, and we began to look for white elm, red oak, and black cherry in the upper forest. All along the trail we kept our field guides open and our eyes continually on the trunks and leaves of the trees. We were alone in the woods, and the openness of the understory made us conscious of how dwarfed we were by the trees.

Eventually, we found ourselves heading back through the mature beech-maple forest, on a broad path that kept us constantly aware of how high above us the canopy hung. We couldn't help stopping a couple of times to link hands and see if the two of us together could ring a trunk—tree hugging taken literally; most often we couldn't. The circuit hadn't really taken us very long, and we weren't eager to move out into a landscape where every place that once had looked like Warren Woods had been leveled and cleared.

When we had been with our family and their neighbors the day before, we had been all too conscious of the passage of time—the block party had been recurring for a quarter of a century, the national holiday two and a quarter centuries, and we couldn't avoid notice of our children's maturing, our elders' passing, our own aging—but in the forest even the national holiday seemed to celebrate the blink of an eye. Some trees in Warren Woods are twice as old as the country, perhaps began growing before Europeans had reached the Great Lakes. Barring the casual and devastating hand of man, saplings already on the ground would replace the tallest trees and make the most of the new millennium. Looking up at the canopy scratching the sky, I was aware of how different a scale the forest used to measure time.

Perhaps Edward Warren knew this too, knew that even if you destroy all the clocks, you will have no effect on the passage of time. Warren Woods is a chronometer with extra hands that encompass in a single tick a human lifetime, a historical era, a century, hands circling the clockface on such a grand scale that no one has seen them move. It doesn't simply give us a window into landscape of the historical past; it isn't simply a memorial commemorating human impact on the environment; it's also an opportunity to replenish a sense of humility about our existence, a reminder of our inevitable place, despite our technology and our intellect, in an enduring and unchangeable natural order.

As conscious of mortality as I had been when I came to Warren Woods, I somehow felt relieved, reassured, by being so small beside the trees, so transitory against the scale of their existence. It took a few more minutes in their shade before we were ready once again to move out into the empty open.

Malabar Farm
(Malabar Farm State Park, Ohio)

I first encountered Malabar Farm in E. B. White's long book review–in–verse. "Malabar Farm is the farm for me," it opens, "It's got what it takes to a large degree." I loved White's jaunty, jovial tone, the merry, rollicking pace as he rhymed elements of Louis Bromfield's book *Malabar Farm*. I somehow knew that, in the second quarter of the century, Bromfield had been both a prolific novelist and a voluminous writer about his farming. I assumed that White had been amused by that dual identity and thought his lively, colloquial style an appropriate match for the earnest energy of Bromfield's book.

In some passages of his 120-line review White details Bromfield's farmwork.

> And every time a field grew fitter
> Bromfield would add another critter,
> The critter would add manure, despite 'im
> And so it went on—ad infinitum.

In others he contrasts both sides of Bromfield's dual existence as farmer and best-selling author:

> Cats in the manger, rats in the nooks,
> Publishers scanning the sky for books,
> Harvested royalties, harvested grain,
> Bromfield scanning the sky for rain.

His rhymes are often startling and funny even as they accurately record Bromfield's activities:

From the Hog Lot Field to the Lower Bottom
The things a farm should have, he's got 'em;
Foe of timothy, friend of clover,
Bromfield gives it a going over,
Adds some cobalt, adds some boron,
Not enough? He pours some more on.

It's a very performable book review, fit for exaggerated declamation.

At the time I chanced on the review, I was reading everything White wrote and, though the center of my interest was his essays, had become familiar with his light verse and his rare reviews. I smiled automatically whenever I leafed past the review in one of his collections but spent no time thinking about the poem or its subject.

Both *Malabar Farm* and White's review in the *New Yorker* were published in 1948, when any reader would have known who Bromfield was and what the book was about. Sixty years later, probably twenty years after I first read the review, I started spending two weeks of the summer in Ashland, Ohio, and learned that Malabar Farm was now a state park about twenty miles away. I immediately remembered White's review, but almost no one to whom I mentioned Bromfield or Malabar Farm seemed to have heard of them. Their change from immediately identifiable cultural terms to unrecognizable referents intrigued me, and eventually I determined to visit the park. I photocopied the poem to take along, treating it like a rare artifact, sort of my little secret.

But at Malabar Farm the secret has been out since 1948; evidence of the review's existence abounds there. The poem has been woven into the fabric of the farm's narrative, integral to it in the way that certain events and certain individuals can't be separated from its story. Though it was no longer my private knowledge, its pace and rhythm reverberated in me throughout my time in the park. So too did my awareness that all those years ago I'd read the review wrong.

• • •

Malabar Farm is the farm for me,
A place of unbridled activity.
—E. B. WHITE

Behind a tractor driven by Lauren, a naturalist in park ranger uni-
form, the wagon for the farm tour leaves the visitor center fully loaded,
older couples and families lining benches within and along its sides.
We leave the pavement to jostle down a grassy track along a cornfield, the stalks higher than an elephant's eye, as high as the roof of
the wagon, this last day of July. My colleague Steve and I, sitting up
front, smell the tractor's diesel fumes more than the fragrance of corn
tassels. Just beyond the cornfield Lauren stops the tractor and comes
back to stand on the wide hitch. She wants to tell us about a huge solitary white oak in a private field across the road. It was featured in
The Shawshank Redemption, and the landowner removed the stone
fence around it, erected by the film crew, because the film's fans de-
stabilized it by carting off souvenir "Shawshank stones." This won't
be the only time we hear about things tangential to Louis Bromfield
and Malabar farm, tidbits that add color to the tour, if not essential
information.

The Bromfield story is ahead of us, where a field hand named Robert chugs off on another tractor across an open grassy field toward a
field of new mown hay beyond. Lauren explains crop rotation, the al-
ternation of cornfields with bean fields; the beans penetrate the soil
deeper than the corn and lay down nitrogen the corn will need when
its turn comes around once more. The yellow mown hay contrasts
with the deep green grasses. Corn's shallow roots would make runoff a problem but for the border grasses holding the soil tightly. Before we set off again, she tells us to notice how the mowing follows
the contours of the land.

Swallows dart and glide and loop above the fields with dazzling
aerodynamics. Small yellow butterflies hover around us, cabbage
white butterflies flutter low, and a large black swallowtail swoops

suddenly out of a field of butternut squash that the farm grows for the benefit of the Richmond County Food Bank.

At a large centennial barn we all dismount and cross the road to a farm market and an artesian well that Bromfield restructured for better farm use. The large brick building towering above the market and well houses the Malabar Farm Restaurant, on the site of a stage-coach stop built in 1821. Johnny Appleseed came to the stagecoach stop and drank often at the artesian well. We are invited to drink, and I do—the water is absolutely clear and deliciously cold.

Back on the wagon we retrace our path, glancing off at grazing cells—fields fenced to keep cattle grazing in a limited space before they chew the grass down and are moved to another cell, then another, then another, and then, once its grass has grown up again, returned to the first cell. Bouncing and swaying, we circle the hay-field; field sparrows dart across our path. In the field where Robert drives the hay baler, we see hay raked up into the baler and watch the bale inch its way to the rear, where it is slanted up and cannoned out into the screened wagon hitched behind it. Sometimes the bales hit the middle of the stack and tumble forward; sometimes their trajectory shoots them to the highest point in the rear. A tremor of excitement ripples across our wagon each time the baler catapults the bale into the air.

We stop again at a small cemetery where Louis and Mary Bromfield are buried among graves of the Schrack family, the people who built the stagecoach stop and a mill on Schwitzer Run. On Bromfield's simple headstone a quotation from *Thanatopsis*, William Cullen Bryant's meditation on death, reads:

To him who in the love of nature holds
Communion with her visible forms, she speaks
A various language.

Lauren doesn't mention it—she tells another colorful story instead, about Celia Rose, a teenager who poisoned her parents and brother, not to kill them but to get them out of the way of her passion for a local boy.

From the cemetery we gaze at Mount Jeez, a high hill in the distance where Bromfield gave visitors a view of Pleasant Valley and Malabar Farm and discoursed on sound principles of agriculture. His farm manager called these talks Bromfield's "sermons on the mount." From what we've learned so far, Bromfield was not only passionate and committed—he was very often right. As the others reboard the wagon, I hang back by Bromfield's grave, copying down what seems like a fitting epitaph.

• • •

Often in distant parts of the world, among strange peoples,
I had awakened to find that I had been dreaming of Pleasant Valley.
—LOUIS BROMFIELD

When Louis Bromfield returned to America in 1938, after a long self-imposed exile in France, he knew exactly where he wanted to go. In "The Return of the Native," a chapter in *Pleasant Valley*, his first book about Malabar Farm, he tells how his childhood in Ohio had haunted him. "I was coming home to a country which I had never really left . . . the only place in the world for which I had ever been homesick." He claimed, "I dreamed constantly of my home country, of my grandfather's farm, of Pleasant Valley. . . . And those dreams were associated with a sensation of warmth and security and satisfaction that was almost physical."

In a later chapter, "The Plan," explaining what he hoped to accomplish by creating Malabar Farm, he rhapsodizes about his grandfather's farm, which he thinks of as "a fortress of security":

On a hundred acres he had raised and educated eight children, strong, healthy, constructive citizens. He had bought little more than salt, coffee, tea, and spices. All else he had produced out of the earth he owned and cherished, and when winter came, there was a great cellar stored with home canned goods and a fruit cellar heaped with apples, potatoes, and all kinds of root vegetables. In the dry cold attic hung rows of hams and flitches of bacon. In that house I ate as well as I have ever eaten anywhere in the world. I knew that he had spent little or nothing upon food for himself, his wife, his eight children, his hired man and girl and all the relations who were always staying in the big house.

Against this ideal picture he contrasted an image of farmers all across the country who "bought the bulk of their food out of cans off shelves in town grocery stores" and decried "one-crop area farms where wheat, or corn or tobacco or cotton grew up to the front door and the farmer's wife bought canned peas and beans in June or July or August."

Bromfield's father had struggled ineffectively to revive farms where the soil was unproductive and depleted of its nutrients, but Bromfield believed that he could revitalize his land through methods he had observed both on his grandfather's farm and in the farming areas of Europe. In the July 13, 1945, entry of "Malabar Journal," a section of *Malabar Farm*, he extolled the effectiveness of mowing, claiming that, on one of his farms, "where the soil had been reduced almost to the texture of cement, a year or two of fallowing in legumes with lime, mowing the legumes and letting them lie on the surface to mulch the hard ground, retain moisture, and finally to be mixed in the soil," had increased production "by as much as five hundred to a thousand percent." White's second stanza begins accordingly, "When Bromfield came to Pleasant Valley / The soil was as hard as a bowling alley," and, after claiming, "The more he fertilized his fields / The more impressive were his yields," concludes: "It proves that a novelist on his toes / Can make a valley bloom like a rose." Bromfield himself recorded that neighboring pastures in midsummer were "burned out, dormant, weedy, and dry while our own pastures are green and almost lush."

Crop rotation, fertilization, contour plowing, cell grazing, soil retention, and strategic irrigation—Bromfield worked to develop ways

of keeping the farm productive and hoped for the kind of self-suffi-
ciency known on his grandfather's farm over forty years earlier. In
the process he became something of an evangelist for "the New Agriculture" and welcomed to the farm anyone who might offer him
new perspectives on what he was attempting or take away ideas they
themselves could profit by. This was the passion that drove Louis
Bromfield, even while he continued to be the prolific, popular, and
prominent novelist he had been before his return to Ohio.

• • •

Malabar Farm is the farm for me,
It's the proving ground of vivacity.
—E. B. WHITE

The farm tour ends at the Big House, a sprawling white structure of
thirty-two rooms that expanded from a farmhouse base by adding
elements borrowed from architecture throughout Ohio. It seems simultaneously like a farm home and a manor house. We all disembark, and Steve and I join those on the house tour by walking to the
front door and crowding into the foyer. A grand piano stands to one
side, a double staircase straight ahead leads away and circles above
us, and on opposite sides, wide passages into the family and guest
areas of the house open up. Sam, the young park ranger leading the
house tour, maps out the path we'll follow, and she immediately reminds us that this was the house in which Humphrey Bogart and
Lauren Bacall were married. We mill around the foyer and the small
rooms for gardening supplies and phonograph recordings and equipment, then step up into the large library in the side of the house reserved exclusively for family.

The room is lined on one side with shelves filled with hundreds of
books originally owned by Bromfield. The authors include familiar
names from the 1930s and 1940s—Fitzgerald, Steinbeck, Thurber,
Sherwood Anderson, and Sinclair Lewis. Bromfield's books are scattered among them; I recognize at once the spine of *Mrs. Parkington*,

familiar from my parents' bookcase. On other walls hang family photographs and framed cartoons from the *New Yorker* testifying to Bromfield's popularity. One Helen Hokinson cartoon has a matronly lady in a bookstore taking a book from a shelf and telling the clerk, "I've decided to give Louis Bromfield a second chance." In a similar cartoon a similar woman in a liquor store looks at a label on a bottle and says to the clerk, "Why, this is one of the things they're always drinking in Louis Bromfield." The library is a testimony to the vigor of Bromfield's literary life.

We aren't allowed into Mary Bromfield's bedroom, accessible from the library, but gaze from the doorway into a bright, spacious room lined with large windows and decorated in pale blue and white colors that make the room seem airy and calm. Mary had rheumatic fever and often retreated to her bedroom after only a little time with the guests who flowed into the house in an endless stream and with whom her husband socialized at length. The room is a mute implication of their private lives.

Sam leads us toward the rear of the house, into an even larger, well-lighted room, Bromfield's study. The walls are all books, and the floor space is dominated by a long, curved flattop desk with bookshelves on the convex side and a kneehole on the concave side. It was a desk especially made for Bromfield, one that, ironically, he was never able to work at comfortably—he was a tall, burly man. His heavy typewriter still sits on a low metal card table before a broad bay window with a view of the garden. Bromfield's low bed (a replica, not the original) abuts a bookshelf wall; a separate box at the foot is where his favorite boxer, Prince, slept. Bromfield was an insomniac, slept little, and always had his work close at hand.

We take the back stairs to the upper level and tour the room reserved for his agent and close friend, George Hawkins, where memorabilia reminds us of films adapted from Bromfield's books and stories or for which he worked on the screenplay. A hallway lined with photos of movie stars and celebrities whom Bromfield knew or who had visited the farm leads us to a series of bedrooms, including those of his three daughters. Then we descend the staircase and get to tour the social area of the house, where guests from New York, Hollywood, and Paris stayed, dinners were served, and parties were held. These are spacious, open rooms that can hold a throng of people.

Here, on one wall, I find the framed original typescript of E. B. White's poetic review of *Malabar Farm*, with a signed note to Mary from "the bard who wrote it, with thanks for the invitation." White seldom wrote reviews, and most of those he did write were about farming books; Bromfield's review was the only one he wrote as a breakneck verse celebration of a book. White's own farming in Maine, though on a smaller scale than Bromfield's, was nonetheless authentic and earnest. He once joked, in a 1943 letter to the editor Frederick Lewis Allen, "That crack about Bromfield being a *real* farmer roused my sporting blood. I will gladly take him on at any time, he to choose the weapons—anything from dung forks to post-hole diggers or 2-ounce syringes for worming sheep." I can find no evidence, despite the invitation—or the challenge—that White ever actually visited Malabar Farm.

Wedding and honeymoon photographs of Bogart and Bacall are scattered throughout the guest area. It is the inescapable celebrity tidbit about the house, even included in publicity about the farm. That social item doesn't obscure for me the evidence of Bromfield's prolific literary productivity, prominence, and presence everywhere on display. But I'm sure what I'll remember most is the autographed typescript of White's *Malabar Farm* review quietly hanging on the wall.

• • •

From far and wide folks came to view
The things that a writing man will do.
—E. B. WHITE

Louis Bromfield was a prolific and successful author in the first half of the twentieth century. Between 1924 and 1951 he published nineteen novels, earning a Pulitzer Prize for *Early Autumn* in 1926 and in 1928 being labeled by *Vanity Fair* as "the most prominent of our younger novelists" and ranked among such promising contemporaries as Ernest Hemingway, Thomas Mann, Sergei Eisenstein, and Pablo Picasso. He also wrote nonfiction, plays, short stories, and screenplays, and his fiction was intermittently the basis for movies. It's not unfair to say that Louis Bromfield was something of a household name for three decades, which is why Helen Hokinson could count on reader recognition when she included his name in a cartoon.

Bromfield regarded his first four novels as "panels" in a series, as if he were arranging a gigantic midwestern polyptych on the scale of a Diego Rivera mural in prose. It was an ambitious project, its panels linked by a recurring theme of a productive pastoral world despoiled by industrialism and commerce. The settings were identifiably backgrounds in and around Mansfield, Ohio, where he grew up. Initially intending to study agriculture and revitalize his grandfather's farm, he was influenced by his mother to veer into the arts and out of Ohio. *The Farm* (1934), according to Bromfield scholar David D. Anderson, is "his best, most-deeply felt," and most autobiographical novel; it "portrays the transformation of the Ohio country from natural wilderness to unnatural wasteland" and "culminates in the life of a young man determined to understand what cannot be reversed and ultimately to escape it in his imagination if not in fact." The novel may have been Bromfield's attempt to close the door on his midwestern past, but it also foreshadowed his return.

Throughout the late 1920s and the 1930s Bromfield lived in France, somewhat apart from the alienated American expatriate community in Paris. In Senlis, a rural community, he kept close to the land. It was only the impending onset of World War II that brought him back to the United States, where the rewards of his writing continued to be lucrative even as he began to pour more and more of his time, his physical energy, and his intellect into Malabar Farm. The success of his books with book clubs and popular reviewers and readers didn't decline, but throughout the 1930s and early 1940s the gap between his critical reputation and his popularity continually widened as elite literary critics found less and less to admire or approve in his writing.

The most scathing attack came from Edmund Wilson in the *New Yorker* in 1944, in a review of *What Became of Anna Bolton* titled "What Became of Louis Bromfield." Wilson calls the novel "a small masterpiece of pointlessness and banality" with "not a single stroke of wit, not a scene of effective drama, not a phrase of clean-minted expression, and hardly a moment of credible human behavior." He tracks Bromfield from his earliest novels, when he was "spoken of as one of the younger writers of promise," to this most recent, sixteenth novel, when "by unremitting industry . . . he has gradually made his way into the fourth rank, where his place is now secure." Perhaps conscious of recent film adaptations of *The Rains Came* and *Mrs. Parkington*, Wilson accuses Bromfield of writing stories easy to make into movies and calls *Anna Bolton* "really sub-literary and proto-film."

It's a very harsh review, bristling with contempt, but, as if to highlight the gulf between the judgment of literary critics and the taste of popular readers, the novel sold well and went into multiple hardbound, paperback, and international editions. But even biographers and critics writing retrospectively about Bromfield's novels don't award him equal status with Ernest Hemingway, his contemporary, or Edith Wharton, a friend and correspondent whose fiction his own more nearly resembles.

To complicate his literary reputation, from the time of his founding of Malabar Farm, Bromfield not only made the farm his priority, of more importance than his fiction, but also began to produce a series of nonfiction works centered on farming, some of them outright manifestos, others mixtures of memoir and polemic. The literary establishment didn't quite know what to make of a best-selling novelist promoting sustainable agriculture from a farm in the middle of Ohio. (In another Helen Hokinson cartoon the caption reads: "I wonder what Louis Bromfield charges for his bacon.") If, as Anderson asserts, *The Farm* is Bromfield's best novel, then a good deal of Bromfield's writing is ultimately an attempt to find his way to the fulfillment that Malabar Farm finally gave him. As a novelist, Bromfield wasn't dedicated either to the aesthetics of fiction or, in spite of his commercial success, to the commerce of fiction. Like many writers, he started out where he was, exploring the concerns most vital to him, exhausting the possibility of finding satisfying resolution to his concerns, and continuing to write almost from habit. By the end of his career—he published his last novel in 1951, his last nonfiction in 1955, and died in 1956—it was his nonfiction that was the most satisfying for him, not for its aesthetics but for its content, which was expressing the ideas and experiences most important to him.

Bromfield himself more than once recorded his own disenchantment with his literary life. In a journal entry in *Malabar Farm* he tells of a young woman "all dressed up and wearing high-heeled shoes" who "had hitch-hiked from Mansfield and wanted to know how to write." Bromfield observed: "Of course there isn't any recipe except to have something to say and to learn how to say it. Nearly always the people who want to 'know how to write' want to be writers not because they like writing or have anything to say but because they think it's a free and easy life with a lot of money—which it isn't, God knows! But it's a poor basis on which to build any success." Bromfield's writing had made him wealthy, and it's telling that he doesn't equate his fame and fortune as a writer with having achieved success.

In one of his final books, *From My Experience*, published the year before he died, he wrote:

> And so in the light of all this, the writing of fiction, unless it was merely a story to divert a tired world or provide relaxation for it, came presently to seem silly. It still does, no matter how pompous, how pretentious, how self-important, how cult-ridden the writer or the product. In this age fiction writing is simply a way of making a living and for my money not a very satisfactory or even self-respecting one. There are better and more satisfying things to do. One degree sillier are the writings of those who write importantly about novels.

The last sentence, perhaps a final, gratuitous slap at the Edmund Wilsons of the world, shouldn't distract us from the sense of Bromfield's own self-awareness in this passage. His real concern, in his final year of ill health, was whether there had been any lasting success in his efforts at farming.

• • •

A book like his is a very great boon,
And what he's done, I'd like to be doon.
—E. B. WHITE

Anne Trubek, the author of *A Skeptic's Guide to Writers' Houses*, claims that the houses of seventy-three American authors are open to the public. In the few I've toured, more by accident than design, I'm often both pleased and disappointed—pleased to get a glimpse of private life for writers I've read, disappointed at how little their artifacts enhance my understanding of their writing. The houses are more cloudy windows into biography than into literature. Though I've read only one of Bromfield's novels, the forgettable *Colorado*, decades ago, and toured the farm inspired mainly by White's review and Ashland's proximity, Malabar Farm prods me into reading around in Bromfield's nonfiction. In time I realize that Malabar Farm makes a more lasting impression on me because the window into biography is clearer here and also because, for Bromfield, biography and literature are essentially the same thing.

It's possible—at least for me—to see E. B. White's spirited and celebratory review of Bromfield's nonfiction in the *New Yorker* as counterbalancing Edmund Wilson's derisive review of Bromfield's fiction in the same magazine four years earlier. White's review may not have restored Bromfield's credibility for the literary community, but it validated his agricultural writing. White maintained his own saltwater farm in Maine on a smaller, less dogmatic, and less ambitious scale than Bromfield did his farm in Ohio—essays such as "The Death of a Pig" as well as *Charlotte's Web* attest to his own authority and comfort as a farm writer—but White was enough of a farmer to appreciate what Bromfield was attempting at Malabar.

Throughout the review White is specific about Bromfield's methods. The contrasts between the hyperactive, frenetic pace of the social life at Malabar and the intensity and tirelessness of the farming make for amusing moments in the poem, but White attends carefully to the agricultural strategies Bromfield applies:

> Most men cut and cure their hay,
> Bromfield cuts it and lets it lay;
> Whenever he gets impatient for rain
> He turns his steers into standing grain;
> Whenever he gets in the least depressed
> He sees that another field gets dressed;
> He never dusts and he never sprays,
> His soil holds water for days and days,
> And now when a garden piece is hoed,
> You'll find neither bug nor nematode.
> You'll find how the good earth holds the rain.
> Up at the house you'll find Joan Fontaine.

The last line somewhat undercuts the attention to farming, but all of those practices are what made Bromfield's farm so interesting and his methods so compelling for the hundreds of farmers who came to visit Malabar Farm and listen to Bromfield expound on them. The ending of the poem is nothing less than an argument in favor of Bromfield's ideas, capped by a personal endorsement of them. White writes:

> I think the world might well have a look
> At Louis Bromfield's latest book;
> A man doesn't have to be omniscient
> To see that he's right—our soil's deficient.
> We've robbed and plundered this lovely earth
> Of elements of immeasurable worth,

And darned few men have applied their talents
Harder than Louis to restore the balance;
And though his husbandry's far from quiet,
Bromfield had the guts to try it.
A book like his is a very great boon,
And what he's done, I'd like to be doon.

This is a generous and considered endorsement of Bromfield's agricultural ideas.

Wendell Berry, himself a respected novelist, poet, essayist, and farmer, once acknowledged reading *Pleasant Valley* and *The Farm* in his youth and claimed to be "grateful for the confirmation and encouragement" they gave him. He added, "At the time when farming, as a vocation and an art, was going out of favor, Bromfield genuinely and unabashedly loved it. He was not one of those bad pastoral writers whose love for farming is distant, sentimental, and condescending. Bromfield clearly loved it familiarly and in detail; he loved the work and the people who did it well."

Bromfield's turn from fiction to nonfiction restored in him a sense of purpose in his writing. The farm books are where his passion and his precision and his lyrical expression surfaced even as he continued to churn out fiction in which he was less and less invested. Only someone who has read all of Bromfield, like the scholar David D. Anderson, has been able to see that the farming books were a continuation of the themes of the early novels and that the later novels were side roads his narrative impulses traveled while his deepest concerns continued throughout his writing in another genre. That his fiction and his nonfiction appealed to different, perhaps very separate, sets of readers and reviewers is less a comment on Bromfield as a writer than on the vagaries of taste and interest and skewed judgment among readers and critics.

Bromfield's fiction may have gone deservedly out of fashion, but his ideas on farming are still viable and relevant. Maybe Malabar Farm is most important not to preserve the memory of a once celebrated author but as a reminder of a flawed but visionary passion we need more urgently than ever. The farmer, the author, and the man were harder to separate from one another in Louis Bromfield.

• • •

Malabar Farm is the farm for me,
It's the greenest place in the whole countree.
—E. B. WHITE

We are reluctant to leave Malabar Farm after the farm and house tours, not willing to take away only impressions, remembered glimpses of reenacted farm activities, of collected and preserved family artifacts. We only have static images of Bromfield, his solid build and steady stance, his sleeves rolled up, his eyes squinting into the sun, his boxers trailing him or clustered around him in the fields, his comfortable familiarity with his tractors. We hope we can add another layer to our sense of place by walking trails in the woodlot Bromfield insisted on maintaining in the southern section of the farm.

The wooded trails give us a glimpse of terrain that wasn't cleared for farming. Preserved for its practical value in firewood and maple sugaring, it not only suggests what the land was like before settlement cleared it but offers a reminder that these rolling hills were shaped by glaciers in the distant past. Low glacial cliffs are exposed along the Doris Duke Woods Trail, named for a portion of the farm that Bromfield needed to sell off and that an heiress-socialite friend purchased and donated back to the farm. One more memorable tangent to the Malabar story.

We seem to have the woods to ourselves. The trail winds uphill through a forest of huge, towering beeches, the forest floor kept open by the shade of the canopy and the decades-long accumulation of leaves. We stop often to examine the width of trunks or gaze upward at the canopy so far above us and, coming out of the woods, walk along a road that reveals the layered glacial cliffs and the creek running at their base on one side and similar rock formations on the opposite side.

Encouraged by a couple we meet on the road to hike to a cave just before the loop on the Butternut Trail begins, we stroll up another road to the trailhead. Soon we're walking on fallen butternuts, through a forest of butternut, maple, and beech trees. The undergrowth on the forest floor is thick and flourishing, and the trail circles an enormous glacial erratic. We climb gradually and see the turnoff for the cave and then the cave mouth straight ahead of us.

At the end of the trail a line of rocks leads us across a rivulet to reach the mouth of the cave. We don't go inside but step up to it to judge how high and deep the cave might run. Light filters into the cave from above, and to find its source we follow the trail farther, around the shoulder of the hill, up to the roof of the cave. Some mild bushwhacking takes us to the crack into the cave. The rock layers here are largely the same composition as the glacial cliffs, and a long fissure has opened across the roof of the cave, a miniature canyon clogged with boulders and shaded by higher moss-covered rocks. The crack isn't very wide; it's jagged and debris filled, and we suspect the cave isn't very deep and is mostly at the base of a cliff face peeling away.

We know from this point that we'll turn back. Steve drifts off to find a rock where he can sit and make notes, and I remove myself a little distance away to a long, thick fallen tree dotted with large outgrowths of fungi, where I scribble a few notes of my own. We are, after all, both writers, though not quite on Bromfield's prolific scale, and it's a fascinating and rugged terrain. Because we're the only ones there, it seems more remote than it really is, and wilder.

Somehow the moment is enhanced by our knowing that the woods we sit in had been Bromfield's. And that's the moment I realize that I'd been resisting my interest in Malabar Farm and accept my pleasure in being here. There's something larger than the preservation of faded celebrity here, the celebration of a local boy who once made good. Here Bromfield has a palpable presence, and it doesn't rest merely on former fame and colorful personality. Sixty-five years after his death, in the era of *The Omnivore's Dilemma* by Michael Pollan and *Animal, Vegetable, Miracle* by Barbara Kingsolver, Louis Bromfield's passions at Malabar Farm seem prophetic, vital, and prescient. It's not hard to imagine that if he were around today, he would be a significant voice in the conversation about our agricultural future, less of a maverick and more of an elder statesman. He faulted himself for his failures on the farm, but he was willing to share the lessons he learned. The most sustainable outcome of his experiment at Malabar Farm may be his writing about land and nature and man's relation to them. That hasn't decreased in value or lost much of its currency.

When we come down out of the woods and the landscape opens up to a view of the Big House and the hay and cornfields, I feel as if I understand Bromfield's passion for Pleasant Valley. I came to Malabar Farm with E. B. White's robust review romping through my brain, but I'll leave sharing his respect for Bromfield's vision and vigor. I hear White's opening line again: "Malabar Farm is the farm for me," and I smile, and then, once more, I say it out loud.

five

Terra Cognita
(Acadia National Park, Maine)

I drive up Cadillac Mountain on the spur of the moment, after a morning at sea level wandering around Great Head and Sand Beach to get a feel for the Maine coastline. I've only just begun my three weeks as an artist-in-residence at Acadia National Park, and I want to orient myself to the terrain. My best chance for that may well be the peak on which the nineteenth-century artist Sanford Gifford painted the vista I'm most familiar with, the view from Cadillac Mountain.

I'm unable to see the mountain from afar today. Hiking the headlands above the shore, I gaze inland from time to time in hopes of a clear view, expecting to see it tower above the nearer, lower mountains. But each time I look, all summits are shrouded in fog. Throughout the day it shifts altitude and thickness, sometimes wispy and translucent, sometimes heavy and dense, but always it envelops the peaks. I'm not certain whether I've seen Cadillac at all. Visibility is reasonably good on the shoreline, though circumscribed; I think that, however limited my vistas may be up there, at least I'll see the summit itself.

When I start up the access road, near sea level, the fog is thin and transparent, but it soon thickens. Within a tenth of a mile it hangs above the road like a banner stretched between bordering trees. It's over three miles to the summit, at 1,530 feet the highest point not only in the park but also along the Atlantic coastline. Soon the trees beyond the shoulder become indistinct, and as I steadily climb, they disappear altogether. I move through an opaque haze, aware only of the pavement. What's beyond the edges of the road, what the occasional turnouts are designed to overlook—these are mysteries. The vehicles ahead make slow progress up the curving two-way road. I can see only the taillights and rear bumper of the van in front of me, occasionally discern the headlights of the car behind. Huffing figures on bicycles suddenly appear and disappear along the edge of the pavement. Off the cliff-edge side of the road, beyond the trees and shrubs immediately marking the shoulder, there is no vista, no view, no horizon. A curtain of thick white vapor rises impenetrably alongside and overhead and yet still thickens.

The caravan I follow eventually slows to a crawl, and we creep into a hazy oval parking lot. I maneuver cautiously into an empty space, get out, and step up onto a paved walkway. I see nothing beyond the walk, no farther into the lot than the trunk of my car. With no idea where to go, I have achieved not orientation but disorientation.

All at once, beyond my car, in a kind of Harry Potter–like moment, a trolley car emerges out of the fog. It draws to a stop, and a tour guide disembarks, followed by a couple dozen passengers. Nothing is visible in any direction. The guide waves his right arm straight ahead into the haze: "We passed the gift shop on the way in and it's off in *that* direction, but"—his arm jerks a little farther to the right—"you should just follow the sidewalk around the lot in *this* direction." Then he waves his left arm off to the other side: "The path that leads to the trail around the summit is over *there*. You won't be able to see anything, but some signs up there will tell you what you would be seeing if it was a clear day." His passengers drift in either direction.

I mingle with those shuffling toward the summit path and soon find myself in a fenced circle where long, low signs illustrate and label outlines of distant islands and mountains as far off as Mt. Katahdin, 115 miles away. So *that's* how far we might see on a clear day. For those looking up from the signs in hopes of a distant reality, it's as if the panorama has been moved indoors and enclosed by encircling white walls. Without the signs or a pocket compass, it's impossible to estimate any direction other than up or down—you can see your feet after all—and we discern only low trees and rocks a dozen or so strides away. All locations look alike, white and cottony, except for where you stand, and if you change location, you can't find any markers to confirm you're in a different place. For all we can tell, we might be at sea level. We are all enveloped in white wet fog, and the limits of our horizons can be measured in feet, hardly more than a few yards. The fog obliterates almost all information that can't be gleaned close at hand, like the green of the low trees and bushes and the lichen-coated, grooved, and rounded rock wherever we walk.

It's a lesson in vision, in the way the sky shuts down the aspirations of the earth. We are in a mist awaiting the reappearance of Brigadoon, completely uncertain of the appointed date and time. We are immersed in an encircling cloud on a foundation of granite bedrock, without recognizable indicators of time or place. We are nowhere.

And Cadillac Mountain? It is nowhere too. It and the island it rises above and the ocean it overlooks—all are gone. Vanished into a dense and all-encompassing fog.

The lure of terra incognita.

For me Acadia National Park was unfamiliar terrain. Having spent my life near the Great Lakes or deep in the midwestern interior, I'd never seen the coast of Maine. Of Acadia I knew only that it took up most of Mount Desert Island, close by the coast. I envisioned its landscape only with postcard or calendar images—coastal forests, rugged cliffs, pounding surf. It made me think of my favorite Latin words: *terra incognita, insula, peninsula*—land unknown, island, nearly an island. I was drawn to the park by these words.

Or so I thought.

It turns out that I have a penchant for visiting the vanished, and here the names of places evoke and commemorate the lost. *Acadia*, for example, from the French *l'Acadie*, a variation on an Abenaki term for "place," or "plentiful place." L'Acadie once encompassed French maritime holdings in Canada, including, before Britain wrested it all away, a portion of Maine. The current name of the park, originally called the Sieur de Monts National Monument and later Lafayette National Park, commemorates a lost French colony.

(Acadia National Park, Maine)   151

When French explorer Samuel de Champlain saw the barren summits of the island, he dubbed it the "isle des monts deserts," the island of barren mountains. Even Anglicized, the name retains its French roots. Strangers from "away" may pronounce the second word "DEZ-ert," as if it were the Gobi or the Sahara, but the locals pronounce it "duh-ZERT," sounding either French or like the English noun for an after-dinner confection or, perhaps more relevantly, the verb meaning "to abandon." Champlain also named Isle au Haut ("Aisle a ho," the high island), where a distant satellite section of the park is located. On Mount Desert a mountain has been named for him, as has another for the Sieur de Cadillac, who once owned all this land under a grant from *le roi de France*; the Sieur de Monts, Champlain's employer, is memorialized by a spring.

Other names allude to earlier inhabitants, the Abenaki, or, in park literature, the Wabanaki. Both terms derive from an Algonquin word for "people of the dawn," or "easterners" (not the name the people of the dawn gave themselves). The Abenaki called the island *Pemetic*, the sloping land; their word *Penobscot* means "rocky place," or "place of ledges." Both names now identify two of the highest "monts deserts."

And then there's Norumbega, the Cibola of the east, a rumored city of fabulous wealth fifteen leagues inland. For a while it lured the adventurous and the opportunistic in vain. One scholar argued it was the site of a Norse or Viking settlement established by Leif Ericson, a claim supported in an old version of the *Columbia Encyclopedia*, which asserts that "probably the word is a Native American version of the old form of Norway." Less imaginative linguistic scholars think it an Abenaki word meaning "quiet stretch of water," or "quiet place between the rapids." No tangible evidence places Vikings among the vanished of Acadia; no site has been uncovered for Norumbega.

More names come from the language of geographers and paleontologists and geologists, a tongue just as exotic and rarefied as a near-lost Native American language. The rocky coastline here, so different from the geology of inland Maine, has been identified as the remnant of Avalonia. The name recalls the misty island of legend where the body of King Arthur reposes. At www.paleos.org/Avalonia we learn that "Avalonia was an Early Paleozoic microcontinent . . . originally part of Gondwana after the breakup of Pannotia in the Neoproterozoic. The Ordovician breakup of the Gondwanan margin generated an archipelago of microcontinents, of which Avalonia was the first to rift away." This language could come straight out of Tolkien or Edgar Rice Burroughs, a geography of Middle Earth perhaps or of Pellucidar or Barsoom. An archipelago of microcontinents indeed. Other plate tectonic theorists think the coastline was part of Eurasia, once joined to North America with the closing of the ancient ocean Iapetus, then separated from it with the opening of the Atlantic. The sites of paleogeography often have the ring of myth and legend.

Avalonia, Pemetic, l'Acadie—simply different kinds of terra incognita, less unknown than perhaps no longer knowable, *terra vanescera*, to coin a phrase, land disappeared. Vanished continents. Vanished oceans. Vanished cultures.

There's more.

Though plate tectonics and ancient oceans affected the bedrock geology of Acadia, glaciers determined much of its surface. Ice sheets of unbelievable thickness and weight scraped what we now call Maine clean down to bedrock, pushed its surface offshore, pressed it down into the crust of the earth. Then the glaciers receded. Relieved of the weight of the ice, the land rose, and ridgetops emerged above the waters; valleys and lowlands remained submerged by rising sea levels. The evidence of glaciers can be found on those bare mountaintops, in the lakes formed by moraine-dammed valleys, in the enormous glacial erratics left high and dry in unfamiliar locales, in the fjord that nearly cuts the island in half. The glaciers themselves, however, are among the vanished.

The glacial retreat opened the anonymous coast to those who would bestow the names: millennia of transient aboriginal groups; centuries of European explorers and settlers; decades of tourists, vacationers, the so-called rusticators. An extremely wealthy elite arrived, bought large tracts of land on which to construct manorial "cottages," and, to prevent Mount Desert from being overrun by development, provided the resources and the incentive to purchase and preserve vast stretches of forested island. They campaigned to create out of their holdings the first national park in the East—still the only one in New England—and accomplished it in 1919. In time the rusticators themselves disappeared, and then, in 1947, fire destroyed two-thirds of their park and most of their cottages. Not only was the society that created the park gone, but what they had left behind and what they had hoped to preserve had vanished too—except for the names.

The names preserve the history of the landscape, tell us what tribes and colonizers and recreationists thought they saw in the terrain, what they hoped to remember of what no longer existed. I wonder whether what remains bears any resemblance to what might have been seen in the distant past. And so I search for a threshold I can cross to travel back in time, a doorway that gives me access to the Acadia of the past.

I return to the summit of Cadillac Mountain on a clear, sunny day. I ascend briskly, still watchful for traffic—the road is never empty—but now aware how the vista expands with the altitude. Rising above an ever-spreading forest, I'm soon high enough to gaze out across the island-dotted waters of Frenchman Bay. At each overlook I pass people parked to record the view with cameras, video recorders, and cell phones. In the turnouts and on the road we all look down on other mountains.

The mountaintops, as Cadillac noted, are more or less bare and open to the sky. The trees grow lower to the ground the higher up I go, spruce and white pine giving way to pitch pine and juniper; at the top the large patches of exposed granite, rounded and grooved, challenge the efforts of plant life to anchor itself. Cadillac Mountain has the only summit in the park accessible by road. From neighboring peaks, such as Dorr Mountain to the east and Pemetic to the west, it's possible to see vehicles laboring up Cadillac's access road and hear their engines straining. Voices of tourists at the peak resound across the distances. On any of those other mountains, their summits attainable only on foot, the person who hears the sounds of Cadillac may, after a solitary climb, be standing on that lower peak entirely alone.

My ascent of Cadillac ends in the parking lot loop just past the busy gift shop. I circle halfway around before I find an empty space.

Paved paths crisscross Cadillac's summit and lead to a point with 360 degrees of panorama, that circle with the low wooden fence and those long rectangles of information pointing out distant locations. Stone steps take visitors to a lower walkway circling the summit, with better viewpoints for gazing off the sides of the mountain. I sling my daypack over my shoulder and amble up to the orientation circle to spend a few minutes comparing shapes on the skyline with shapes on the signs. Then I set off for a particular location, the site of Sanford Gifford's painting *The Artist Sketching on Mount Desert, Maine*.

I carry in my daypack a copy of Pamela J. Belanger's profusely illustrated book *Inventing Acadia: Artists and Tourists at Mount Desert*, a companion volume to an exhibition she curated at the Farnsworth Art Museum in Rockland, Maine. Her premise is that landscape artists who painted on Mount Desert raised awareness of the island in the mid- to late nineteenth century, giving rise first to the tourist industry, then to the "cottage" community, and ultimately to the national park. To demonstrate a symbiosis in the relationship between painters and tourists, she notes that color photographs on postcards from Mount Desert Island in the twentieth century often reproduced what Thomas Cole, Frederic Church, and Sanford Gifford had painted in the nineteenth. The popular sites for visitors to the island usually were those they were already familiar with through paintings and guidebook illustrations. In that way art established what in nature was worthy of being beheld, and in turn the popularity of those sites both confirmed the judgment of the artists and also established the need for those sites to be accessible.

Because a considerable portion of Mount Desert Island had been set aside and encroachment on it by lumber and resort industries had been forestalled by the creation of the national park, I wonder if some of the original scenes might still be available for viewing; that is, if somewhere on the island the landscape of the painter might *still* be the landscape of the tourist. The cover of *Inventing Acadia* displays a detailed section of Gifford's *Artist Sketching*, painted around 1864–65; the entire painting is reproduced later in the book. My goal today is to compare the picture with the actual site where it was painted.

In Gifford's painting the viewer is looking roughly due south from the summit of Cadillac Mountain. The top third of the painting displays a broad band of brownish haze across the sky and a narrower band of hazy blue, the Atlantic Ocean, below it. The bottom two-thirds depict forested land stretching out below Cadillac Mountain to the coast. Otter Cove, a light blue finger poking down into the hazy green of the forest, interrupts the uppermost line of the land, and a couple of houses in the settlement of Otter Creek and a short section of road are visible in tiny openings in the otherwise unbroken woodland. The south ridge of nearer, lower Dorr Mountain, a darker green than the lowlands, its conifers more distinctly rendered, takes up the left foreground corner. A rocky slope on Cadillac Mountain, a rugged extension of the summit, fills the nearer foreground in the bottom right. The viewer sees here a figure seated at the edge of a rock, bracing a sketchbook or small canvas on his knees. Behind him an open sketch box displays a completed painting of the view from that rock inside its raised lid. Beyond the sketch box are a closed sunshade and possibly a campstool. The long inclined boulder the artist sits on is anchored at the bottom by another, upright boulder with a very distinctive formation, a weathered pyramidal point, jutting out of its upper right side. The slope on which he sits lifts him just right of center in the picture, so that the viewer simultaneously sees the view he's sketching and also watches him observe the landscape. White sailboats on the sea and in the cove and white houses in the forest are the only hint of civilization beyond the presence of the artist himself.

As the highest point, Cadillac Mountain was established early as the most significant viewing area on the island. Pamela Belanger quotes an 1886 guidebook to the island: "the two grandest objects in nature, high mountains and a boundless ocean, here occupy the same horizon, and no earthly view can be more absorbing." Gifford's painting of the vista justifies that judgment.

I move slowly around the southern face of Cadillac Mountain's summit, Belanger's cover picture in my hand, keeping Otter Cove as my point of orientation and trying to line myself up at the angle that the viewer of the painting is presumed to have. I manage to align the coastline but can't seem to locate the foreground of Gifford's painting. I remember that, though Belanger makes a point about postcards replicating Gifford's painting, the example she provides is no more successful at exactly replicating his point of view than my efforts are.

I open Belanger's book to the full picture of *The Artist Sketching* and notice one of his earlier sketches from Mount Desert on the facing page. Though the landscape portrayed in that picture isn't specified, it looks to me very like the view north from the summit of Pemetic Mountain. I'm struck by the similar composition of both paintings, each a view from on high with a forested center and the lower right-hand corner taken up by a rocky slope. In both pictures the rocky slope is nearly the same, each anchored by the same upright boulder with a pyramidal point on its right side. Though the center and background of both paintings are more or less identifiable, it's questionable whether that rocky slope in the foreground of each picture exists in either location or, for that matter, whether it exists anywhere at all. Certain it is that Gifford has transposed it from one painting to another. As true to the view from Cadillac Mountain as *The Artist Sketching* may be when it comes to Otter Cove and that portion of the southern shoreline of Mount Desert, the foreground is at best an embellishment. Gifford records Mount Desert in the background and "invents Acadia," in Belanger's term, in the foreground.

I make a rectangle of my raised hands, thumbs touching, fingers up, and shift them before my eyes, searching for an approximation of Gifford's frame. The light green forest fills the middle ground, topped by the bright blue of the Gulf of Maine and the Atlantic Ocean and, above that, the paler blue of a nearly cloudless sky. Otter Cove and the modern causeway across it as well as portions of a road and a few scattered buildings are visible through the trees in approximately the same location where Gifford placed them in his painting. I notice two offshore islands, not exactly where Gifford's are but close enough to seem identifiably the same. The sun is higher overhead for me, the scene everywhere brighter, the shadows not so dark as in Gifford's painting. My foreground, just above my thumbs, is made up of slabs of rock of differing shades of gray, none of them distinctly upright with a pyramidal point. Shifting my perspective vertically, I take in a little more of the foreground and remind myself how bald the summit is. *Monts deserts*—mountains barren of trees and shrubbery except for low bushes in the places between the boulders and gray granite slabs.

It's a beautiful vista, that's for certain, though not quite as precipitous as Gifford suggests—he seems to have elevated the angle at which the painter sketches and the viewer sees the whole—and it provides a magnificent view of the coastline, "high mountains and a boundless ocean." Except for adjustments and additions I've already mentioned, the view replicates Gifford's closely—the same sense of scope and scale, the distant ocean boundless beyond the horizon, the mountain high enough to give a sense of altitude and distance. Here, fully, is the opportunity for the "magisterial gaze," as the art historian Albert Boime termed it, the proprietary sense of being master of all you survey.

With so much of what humans have done on and to Mount Desert Island invisible or vanished, reduced by time or scale from this perspective, it's possible to strip all of the layers of cultural superimposition away and think that what you behold is the landscape itself. Immersed in *civilization* as we are, we have difficulty seeing nature without the intervening scrim that civilization provides; immersed in *nature*, we still find the scrim hanging before our eyes. Even if I lacked a knowledge of the history here, even if Gifford's painting were unknown to me, would I not think that what I behold is a view,

Terra Cognita

a panorama, a subject for photographs and en plein air painting, particularly on a day when the sky is tinted blue and white and the sea is a brilliant ultramarine and the forest a range of vibrant greens and the rocks pink-tinged gray speckled with green and black lichens and the few people anywhere in the view are miniscule in the scale of the landscape? How "magisterial" would my gaze be if I were the first person to stand on this summit and survey this terrain when it was truly unknown to other men?

Luckily, I can usually raise that scrim or look around it. Rather than feel a sense of mastery over the landscape, as the term *magisterial* implies, I am most often inclined to let the view dominate me. To stand on a mountaintop, gazing out on a limitless ocean, off across a vast continent, doesn't make me feel in control of anything. Instead, I'm likely to accept my lot as an infinitesimal part of an unimaginable immensity and simply hope, in some way, to feel connected to it.

But at the moment I feel neither magisterial nor minute, only solitary and cut off, as if I had been vainly trying to commune with the ghost of Sanford Gifford. The view from Cadillac Mountain seems no clearer to me than when I approached it through the fog. I still don't feel as if I know where I am.

I climb Cadillac Mountain again, the old-fashioned way this time, up the south ridge of the mountain. My starting elevation is around 175 feet above sea level, and in three and a half miles I'll gain over 1,300 feet. The trail begins in thick forest, shaded and dark, mostly tall white pine and spruce, and rises gradually. The short starting stretch is easy going, but here, where soil cover is shallow on glacier-scoured bedrock, the footing quickly becomes uneven. I tread warily over tree roots and cobblestones, watching my feet most of the time but trying to glance across the open forest floor as I advance.

In a few minutes I overtake a family group farther up the trail. Their pace is determined by a white-haired woman moving stiffly. She seems frail and hesitant. To one side a girl of eleven or twelve, lithe and eager, watches a middle-aged man, no doubt the woman's son and the girl's father, put a hand under the woman's elbow. He glances at the girl before checking the woman's footing. The girl is expressionless. I briefly wonder about the family dynamics, appreciating how the man has to negotiate his mother's lack of dexterity and his daughter's abundance of energy, a man in the middle. I pass them with an exchange of polite murmurs. I think, as I hurry on, how challenging the rough footing I keep tripping over must be for the old woman, and I wonder how far the three of them will get. About a mile from the trailhead I take a side loop toward Eagle's Crag and find myself scrambling over a few massive boulders; one of my guidebooks recommends this turnoff as an easy family destination, but I think the stone wall I clamber up with effort will likely pose problems for the family behind me, if this is where they're heading.

Eagle's Crag is only a mile from the trailhead and looks down on Otter Creek and out on the Atlantic. By the time I reach it and get my bearings from the view, I notice the forest giving way to open space. Short stretches of exposed granite with stunted spruce and pine growing in the clefts soon turn into longer stretches of bedrock; once I rejoin the main trail, I am well out of the forest, exposed to azure skies, sea breezes, sunshine, and plenty of chances to gaze off across the forest and the lesser mountains and the ocean. The trees are low to the ground, pitch pine shaped by wind and water like, as one guidebook suggests, a Japanese bonsai garden. Despite the angle of ascent, I enjoy having solid rock beneath my feet and breathing the mingled forest and ocean smells in the air. Farther up, I encounter jack pines. Then, at the end of a long hump of granite, I discover the Featherbed, an unusually high boggy area, lush and green, protected against wind deep in a wide flat crevice. I climb down into the declivity, inhale marshy odors as I cross the space, then climb up the granite wall on the opposite side. From the rise out of the Featherbed the trail crosses long stretches of bare rock fringed with low shrubs and occasional outbursts of spruce and fir. I move ever upward over smooth stone, enjoying openness to sun and sky and breeze and long views of my destination. Only when I find a nearly barren tree

Terra Cognita

aflame with a small flock of cedar waxwings in the morning sun do I slow my steady pace.

At the summit I drift around the walkways. I try again to approximate Gifford's perspective as closely as I can, then try to identify islands in Frenchman Bay and locate the mountains of the mainland. Though I have my daybook, sketchpad, and camera in my daypack, I'm content to mosey and gaze. I buy a granola bar in the gift shop and find a rock with a view of Otter Cove where I can eat, sip water from the bottle warming in my pack, and sit idly. I try not to think about what I'm looking at but, rather, hope to somehow absorb the view, as if sitting in the sun will trigger some philosophical photosynthesis in me. It doesn't. Eventually, I rise and set off for the trail back down the south ridge.

By now it's late morning. The waxwings have moved on. I pass more people ascending the trail than I saw when I hiked up. Occasionally, we nod to one another or exchange a few words—a lot of commiseration and encouragement passes among strangers on mountain trails—but otherwise I fall into a familiar trail rhythm, maintaining a constant pace that I automatically renew after each momentary halt to let the upwardly mobile pass. Trail rhythm is akin to a walking meditation, if you can keep your life off the trail off your mind.

Any en plein air essayist will recognize the spirit of Thoreau in that notion. It was Thoreau, in "Walking," who berated himself while in the woods for being preoccupied with his worldly concerns rather than with his physical location; he accused himself of letting his mind be "not where my body is,—I am out of my senses. In my walks I would fain return to my senses." It's a trickier thing to accomplish than it should be. I've taken woodland walks with little awareness of where I've been, my mind so centered on other things that the terrain I pass through is invisible. From time to time, if I'm lucky, I remember to ask myself Thoreau's own question, "What business have I in the woods, if I am thinking of something out of the woods?" On the good walks I don't have to remember the question because somehow my trail rhythm has let my mind be where my body is. So here, descending the south ridge of Cadillac Mountain, I feel the granite through my shoes, hear the chickadees and sparrows in the junipers, see the line where sky and ocean meet, smell the pines, taste the afternoon air. I return to my senses.

Just as I climb out of the Featherbed, I'm startled to encounter the family trio again, farther up the mountain than I thought they'd get and making good time. They recognize me as well, and we stop to chat. The man and the girl stand aside to let the woman do all the talking. We exchange obligatory pleasantries about the day, and then she confides that she turned eighty not long ago and that this family hike is her first trail outing since having artificial joints— "Titanium," she tells me— installed in her left leg. I wonder, but don't ask, if a seven-mile hike over rough terrain with changes in elevation of 1,300 feet going up and coming down is the kind of exercise her doctor recommended for limbering up. As if she reads my concern and feels obliged to allay it, she lets me know she's accustomed to more rigorous hiking. "I usually hike in Vermont or in the White Mountains," she says; "I've climbed Mount Washington." I'm impressed and say so—at 6,288 feet Washington is the highest peak in the eastern United States, four times the elevation of Cadillac and celebrated for having the worst weather in the world and the highest surface wind ever recorded. Immediately doubtful of my own resilience and stamina in comparison, I silently chide myself for past patronizing thoughts. We wish each other good hiking the rest of the day, I wave to the man and the girl, and we separate.

Thoughts of that nameless woman keep me from returning to my senses. I meet a light but steady stream of hikers coming up, many of them overweight and out of shape and, even without newly installed titanium joints, not well conditioned for the hike, but I encourage them when I can. Recalling the trolley and the crowded parking lot, I think: You can reach the summit in easier ways than by walking steadily upward for three and a half miles, if all you're interested in is the view from Cadillac Mountain.

For my own purposes I've made a point of achieving that view, but despite having fixed it in my mind by studying paintings, post-cards, and photographs and surveying it on site, when I try to reproduce the image in my brain, I notice the edges already blurring, details already fallen away. The farther I get from the moment I was there, the less specific the image will become. At the same time I realize that, as ephemeral as that moment was, I have no regrets about being there or, for that matter, about stumbling over the rocks and tree roots of the forest I'm in.

Nor, I'm certain, does that nameless woman approaching the summit with her son and granddaughter. Long past the time her body has told her, "It's okay if we don't do this anymore," she still climbs mountains. To her granddaughter, roughly an eighth as old as she is, the grandmother's eight decades must seem interminable; to the grandmother they must seem to have gone by in the blink of an eye, a single tick of a cosmic watch. Surely in that eighty-year span, if her insistence on taking the long way up Cadillac Mountain is any clue, she must have seen any number of magnificent views. If fleeting accomplishments in an ephemeral life truly counted, she would not have to be on the trail today. She has summitted Mount Washington, after all.

I have expended much time and effort not merely to witness for myself the panoramic view from the summit of Cadillac Mountain but also to survey the long view of the coast of Acadia across time. But I haven't put quite enough effort into witnessing the present moment in the forest where I am. As I keep straining to gaze out across the past, I have to remember that epochs of time are like blankets of fog. They seem to enclose and define the terrain but are really insubstantial and transitory; they burn off, evaporate, in the sun of succeeding days. Note to self re cosmos: It doesn't matter how long it lasts, it will burn off; it will vanish as if it had never been. What can this mean for us whose lives are more fleeting than an ice age, than a tribal history, than a colony, than a park? Perhaps it has something to do with being in the moment, with taking every opportunity to return to your senses.

Terra incognita. Terra vanescera. A place does not become *terra cognita*, known land, when it's named. We know it only when we're on it, move through it, return to our senses in it. Even on a clear day we can't see where we are if our eyes are closed, our senses turned off. We—I—keep needing to relearn how to locate ourselves. The point of reaching the summit is not to recapture the past or to employ the magisterial gaze—it's to be where we are in the present moment, even if it's nowhere we can name.

Time and Tide
(Acadia National Park, Maine)

> The shore is an ancient world, for as long as there has been an earth and sea there has been this place of the meeting of land and water. Yet it is a world that keeps alive the sense of continuing creation and of the relentless drive of life.
>
> —RACHEL CARSON, *The Edge of the Sea*

i. Fog

Four thirty on a cool afternoon, early September. In my second week of residency on the Schoodic Peninsula, the easternmost section of Acadia National Park, I'm paying more attention to the fog than I did last week. Schoodic Point, the tip of the peninsula, is a low, fractured, rocky slope, mostly pink granite interrupted by a few thick stripes of black diabase dike, jutting into the ocean. Most days the point appears like the clear, bright, colorful image I imagined as I flew here from the West: light stone blocks contrasting with vivid green firs on its inland edge; scruffy, light green grasses rising tenaciously from crevices; cobalt blue sea; cerulean blue sky. Down close to the shoreline the intertidal zone begins. Wet, dark, olive green rockweed coats the lowest portions of the slope; the pinkish gray rocks above the limits of high tide stay bare and dry. I stand in sun and sea breeze, studying the cracks and joints and fissures, the angles and shapes of slabs and blocks and shelf faces. I note changes in tide level, the shift from zone to zone—dense, dark green waterlogged weeds; light green weeds draining seawater; damp off-white coatings of barnacles; the glistening, deceptively slick black zone. Sea and sky, those vast blue reaches immeasurable, draw my attention only to their immensity rather than to any fixed point. Each time I return to the point in sunshine, I become pleasantly detached. I'm content with the scale and scope of what I behold and find it easy to simply engage in idle observation.

But the fog—that's something else. It alters my sense of the world, makes me feel both isolated and involved.

Clouds that have hung above the peninsula since morning drift out to sea and the ground-level fog thins in the afternoon sun. I wander out across the rocks, closer to the ocean, hoping for a better perspective on the shoreline, and stop at an abrupt drop-off, a broad break in the granite ledges. Rockweeds glisten in the refracted sunlight, thickly coating slabs and blocks ten feet below me; waves surge in from time to time to cover them, then ebb away. The fog merges with the ocean a little way out. The horizon is only a broad smear of bright blue-gray, except for a short stretch of gleaming silver just below the place where the sun, unseen, must hover. The thickness of the fog shrinks and swells like the surf, like the sea breathing in and breathing out. When it dissipates slightly, the distant silhouette of Mount Desert Island, across the broad reach of Frenchman Bay to the east, momentarily materializes out of the haze, then blurs and blends back into it again.

On the other side of this little inlet where I stand, seven gulls stand placidly near the shoreline; it's as if they're marking time, waiting for the tide to turn and reveal the vulnerable life-forms of the tide pool. Farther inland, upslope toward the landward end of the inlet, a raised lip at the far edge of a granite slab forms a partial dam above an area of lower rocks. The tide must rise and surge across the slab before it can fill up that inner pool and drown those rockweed-coated blocks again. I hear a thump and splash as saltwater spills over the lip. The gulls are silent, immobile. The only sounds are lapping waves, the slap of water on stone, the gurgle of water sucking itself back away from land.

The encircling fog, gradually increasing its distance from the shore, still closes in the horizon. I begin to comprehend the limits of my vision, strain to remember what is usually clear to me in sunlight. I suddenly realize that if I wanted a place to lose myself, to momentarily step out of identity and obligation, it would be here and now. In this instant—perhaps only for an instant—I come wholly to my senses. Cognition ebbs away; feeling surges in. All at once my senses connect me to the most primal of elements—the soft enshrouding fog, the persistent rhythm of the waves, the implacable rock under my feet. In the distance a raft of eiders silently floats by, black shapes interrupting the gleam of sunlit waves, soundless, drifting, carried along by the tide and the waves. I feel myself drifting with them. I am no longer on the Schoodic Point I know but some other where.

I don't know how long the moment lasts or why I feel I need to leave—to "get about my business," whatever that might be—but the moment haunts me, draws me back a few hours later. The sun is descending, the fog thickening, that inner pool slowly filling, other sightseers mostly gone. I am, for the moment, alone on Schoodic Point. I shiver occasionally in a brisk cold breeze. Directly above me, I discern blue sky, but on the ground I find my horizon still tightly circumscribed. Ahead of me sea soon dissolves into fog; behind me, inland beyond the point, trees are merely a frontline of shadows, growing dimmer, the forest beyond it vanished. Clouds high overhead only hint at the sun's descent. No gleam shows through the fog.

I concentrate on what encircles me; I close my eyes and listen to the surf, the slap and gurgle and s-s-s-s of waves against and across and retreating from the rocks. The air is palpable on my face, a chilly damp caress. I conjure up the image of Correggio's painting of Io and Zeus, a naked nymph welcoming the embrace of the god in the guise of a cloud. I smile blindly into the fog, then banish the image to return to my senses. Minutes pass in the grasp of sensation, while cold seeps into me. It's the pervading cold that makes me finally open my eyes. Blinking, I slowly take one last look around me, then surrender the point to the fog, the surf, and the gathering dark.

(Acadia National Park, Maine)

ii. Crossing the Bar

The boreal coast of the North Atlantic is known for the amplitude of its tides, the difference between high and low tide. The intertidal or littoral region is the area of shoreline between what the highest tides submerge and what the lowest tides expose; it can be divided into five distinct zones, each demarcated by degrees of submersion and exposures, each host to a variety of specially adapted organisms. Any casual idler along the coast of Acadia is likely to notice the changes that the levels of the tide make in the appearance of the shoreline.

On the Schoodic Peninsula, for example, depending on the time of day, East Pond Cove seems to be different each time I pass it. At one time it is a broad, serene pond, a beachless basin almost surrounded by higher ground. Its grassy shoreline is close to the road; only a narrow strip of gray rock shows between the water and the pavement. This is the cove at high tide. At another time, at low tide, it is startlingly transformed. Now is revealed a broad stretch of exposed shoreline, little pools of water in between cobblestones and small boulders. A burble of flowing water can be traced to a temporary tidal stream draining the higher sections of the pool. The water's edge is now perhaps twenty yards distant from the shoulder of the road. On the open shoreline, among small exposed rocks all high and mostly dry, are strewn the blue shells of mussels, the empty shells of snails, and billions upon billions of barnacles, the seams of their intricate interlocking plates tightly sealed. Bladder wrack, a rockweed with heart-shaped brown bladders, lies flat everywhere, as if discarded. Abundant, opportunistic gulls peck among the wrack. Across what remains of the water, on the exposed shore of Little Moose Island, a clammer cruises the coastline, probing at the sand and occasionally plucking something out to deposit in the bucket carried on a strap over his shoulder.

It seems a zone of debris and detritus, everything dead—certainly the litter of mussel shells, snail shells, and an occasional dismembered crab suggest abundant death—but most of it will revive with the turn of the tide. The rockweed will rise and stand waving in the water; the barnacles and mussels will open to feed; the periwinkles and whelks will set into predatory motion. At high tide the following day the cove is a placid pool once more, reflecting the sky and suggesting nothing of the abundant life at its bottom. The passerby who observes these changes feels he shares a secret with the landscape and remains conscious of the tides wherever he goes in Acadia.

Bar Harbor is the name of both a harbor and a picturesque town on the eastern coast of Mt. Desert Island, where the main section of Acadia National Park is located. The harbor extends out into Frenchman Bay between two small islands and a somewhat larger island due north a quarter-mile offshore of the town. At high tide Bar Island, the largest of the three, seems simply to be the nearest island, across a relatively calm and sheltered body of water. It's only at low tide that it becomes apparent how harbor, town, and island all got their names.

Twice a day at high tide, for several hours at a time, Bridge Street leads down the slope from the town directly into the water of the harbor. It seems to offer only water access. It's low tide now. As I stroll down the street, a pickup truck passes me near the bottom of the slope and continues out into the harbor, onto a firm, flat tidal bar the width of a two-lane highway. When the ebbing tide drains away the water in that part of the harbor, the flats turn into a packed gravel strand solid enough to support a van or suv, and tourists and townies alike set out to wander across the bar.

I see ahead of me other people already walking idly on the bar. Two long vans park close to the water on the west side of the bar, one of them towing a partly empty trailer for kayaks. Off in the low pool beyond the vans floats a cluster of kayakers, facing each other and holding position with their paddles, apparently returning from an outing on the bay. Not far away a small sailboat heels over in the shallow water, more aground than afloat. Two small station wagons drive briskly across the bar; they pass an older couple ambling back toward town. Groups of people pick their way along the water's edge, surveying the tide line. A little girl, walking several yards ahead of her mother, calls back to her that she sees a starfish. "It's feeding," she shouts. On either side of the bar the tidal flats are cluttered with seaweed, blue mussels by the millions, barnacles in both their closed and their extended states, innumerable periwinkles, and various other tidal creatures.

Midway across the bar I stop and slowly survey everything around me. To the south the flats slope off gradually, and some water-filled areas separate ridges of shells; in the distance, where the harbor is still deep enough, small boats float gently at anchor or move slowly between docks and open water. To the north, where Mt. Desert Island arches toward the mainland, the slope is less pronounced, and the waters have receded less. At either end of the bar, toward the town or toward the island, small figures amble unhurriedly and small vehicles either recede in the distance or grow larger with increasing nearness. The top of the bar is as flat and worn as an old dirt road, but beyond its edges vast fields of innumerable gray-brown mussel shells fall off to the limits where water still covers them. It looks as if the retreating tide has revealed an unimaginable accumulation of lifeless debris, the discarded residue of centuries, yet I'm aware that much of what I'm seeing—and what I can't see beneath the surface in the shallows—is alive, tightly sealed against desiccation from heat and air and exposure, waiting for full submersion before opening up to life again.

Life in the littoral, literally unlimited. Here on the bar I glimpse something of the scale of life in the intertidal zone.

I decide to step along briskly, to complete my tour of the island before the tide turns. The trail leads off the bar and winds through the woods of the island. It closes off the view of the harbor but ends a quarter-mile later at a summit with an open view toward the south. Some prominent mountains of eastern Acadia National Park— Cadillac, Dorr, Champlain—fill the space between cloudy white sky and forested coast. Lower still I see Bar Harbor and its marina, with a couple dozen boats anchored off shore. The harbor looks calm and deep, but when I lean out a little, I can see off to my right the limits of exposed harbor floor and the places where people are walking and driving across the harbor.

Returning to the sandbar, I realize the tide was still ebbing when I first crossed it. The sea is even lower now, revealing the tidal life to be even more endlessly abundant. As far as I can see from sea level, the surface of the harbor bottom is now exposed. Only occasional low pools are still partly water filled, where blue mussels poke only their tips into the air. The van with the trailer, now loaded with kayaks, stands where it did, a few of the kayakers milling around it. The second van has already left with its passengers. The shoreline has retreated farther; the place where the kayakers floated together is nearly completely land. The sailboat is utterly aground, canted to one side and resting on its keel on mud and mussels, no open water anywhere around it.

The image of an exposed harbor floor dense with mussels and barnacles is a revelation to me. For the moment it looks drought ravaged or like land drying out from a sudden torrential rain; it looks as if it has been devastated and will take years to recover. But I know the recovery begins within the hour, and within six hours it will all be submerged, the way I have most often seen it, as if it never could be drained—how do you drain the ocean? Here is life on a scale that staggers comprehension, here is resiliency of a resourcefulness that bewilders invention, here are life forms utterly unlike what we know on land, what we know of our own evolution, whose origins outdate ours by immeasurable millennia.

"Time and tide wait for no man," it is said, but I think that expression a rather benign and banal reading of what we behold here. Instead, time and tide give us some inkling of what eternity must be like, even as, twice a day, they display for us what, ultimately, existence is like. To understand life we need a more panoramic perspective, a slower shutter speed, a more encompassing comprehension. I recross the bar slowly, still looking all about me. I know that all this will soon disappear beneath high water, a fecund existence spending half its time submerged and invisible. To recapture this sight, I will need to time my return with another turning of the tide.

(Acadia National Park, Maine)   171

iii. Cobblestones

It's nearly noon. I'm hiking on Isle au Haut, the remotest section of Acadia National Park. I've rounded Western Head, one of the peninsulas on the southern tip of the island; I've dawdled awhile over an energy bar and bottled water on a rounded bulge of volcanic rock, where I appreciated the good sense of the gulls to have their picnic lunches of crab on top of it—whitening shells beyond counting suggest how often they use it; I've sat contentedly in sea breeze and warm sun, gazing out at the vast openness of the Atlantic. To complete my circuit of Western Head, I've followed the Cliff Trail high above the shoreline on the east side of the peninsula. Now I'm nearing the end of the trail, at its junction with the road that will take me back north to the ranger cabin where I'm staying.

The trail descends to an open rocky beach. I try to distinguish among the stones the marker cairns that will keep me on the trail. Two prominent stone piles steer me away from the shore, back into the trees, but a glance toward the water makes me hesitate before starting inland. A dozen or more cairns have been carefully constructed upon the side of a knob of rock close to the shore. Some are layered like a toddler's stacking toy, decreasing in size from bottom to top; others are more haphazardly arranged and more precariously balanced. I see at once that they are not trail markers, since they would lead me back the way I came, along the bottom of the cliffs. I recall walking on Monhegan Island, farther down the coast of Maine, along a trail through old-growth pine forest, where hikers can discover a string of "fairy" dwellings, miniscule "houses" of twigs, bark, stones, and moss erected at the base of trees; I think that here Isle au Haut seems to counter that idle playfulness with a simpler and rather repetitious sea nymph or mermaid sculpture gallery. The cairns add only whimsical clutter to an already driftwood- and debris-strewn coast, but they prompt me to look back along the sheer cliffs toward the tip of Western Head. I realize more fully what I've been walking above.

Cobblestones make up the walking surface from higher up on the beach, where the forest begins, down to the shoreline, and they fill

in the spaces between the higher, raised knobs of the rocky headlands. They make for noisy, off-balance walking; finally on a beach
for the first time since I arrived on Isle au Haut, I clatter and lurch
across a long stretch of them to get closer to the water. I can tell that
the tide is coming in. Once I stop moving and stand gazing at the
cliffs, I hear other noises than the clacking of the stones under my
feet. I stumble toward the shore, pause, and listen more intently. In
a moment or two I realize that, after an incoming wave, when the
waters recede, I'm hearing the clatter of cobblestones. I step even
closer to the water and stare at the foamy waves covering the lowest
stones. This time I see some of them move as the waters withdraw.
I continue watching and soon notice that the chattering sound of
stones knocking together is louder when the waves are stronger and
heavier. Taking a few steps forward onto wet stones, I squat down,
getting nearer eye level with the stones and the waves. I concentrate
on the cobblestones even when they're invisible under the breaking
waves, camouflaged by white foam. The water recedes off the glistening stones as a wave twenty yards offshore curls above a low bar-
rier of rock. Then the space in between fills with white turbulence.
One wave rushes up almost to my feet and reminds me that this is
a rising tide. I wobble backward across the cobblestones to a stretch
of sloping solid rock and perch on the edge, still focusing my hearing on the clacking sound of the stones.

The tide comes in farther onto the shore and, as it deepens, hits the
stones more heavily. Now when it pulls back, it draws more power-
fully on the stones, and the volume of the clatter increases. The racket
the ebbing water and the rolling stones make together sounds like a
heavy flow of rainwater gushing down a storm drain mixed with the
rattle of thick chains striking against each other. The stronger waves
pick up small stones and hurl them farther back on the beach, and
sometimes they toss up hollow stem kelp as well. The whomp and
whoosh of the waves and the cracking and chittering of the cobbles
grow more forceful. I'm alone on the beach, not a bird or other creature visible, and yet the rocks themselves are active.

(Acadia National Park, Maine)

The moment reminds me of an essay by Barbara Hurd, "Fine Distinctions," in which she walks a shingle beach in southwest Suffolk, on the Atlantic shore of England. She tells how on that site the U.S. military constructed a massive listening device, "the world's largest, most sophisticated, most powerful radar of its kind," at a cost of a hundred million dollars, but soon found it wouldn't work. As she explains, "Its ability to receive signals was, from the start, hampered by the presence of a mysterious noise. 'Clutter-related noise,' they called it. 'Severe background noise,' 'excessive noise of undetermined origin.' Months of testing failed to find the source of the problem." Apparently, none of the project's military and technical personnel had ever sat on a cobblestone beach during an incoming tide. It's not surprising that all that sensitive equipment couldn't overcome the interfering rumble and clatter of wave-tossed cobblestones; but it's discouraging to know that no one involved had predicted the result.

"Shingle pebbles aren't silent," Barbara Hurd says; "they ping and clatter and clunk." Just so. Days after I leave Isle au Haut, a woman will tell me that she can identify which beach she's passing in the dark by the sounds the cobblestones make, differentiated in tone and pitch by the angle of the waves, the slope of the shore, the size of the stones. In *At the Sea's Edge* William T. Fox has a useful chart distinguishing the rocks on the shore. Boulders are the largest rocks; cobbles are grapefruit sized; pebbles are the size of Ping-Pong or golf balls; granules are pea sized. Smaller than that are the coarse, medium, and fine grains of sand and below that silt and clay. These are handy distinctions.

For the most part the waves have been juggling peas and Ping-Pong balls, but just now higher waves are tossing lemon- and peach-sized cobblestones up onto the rocky ledge a few yards from where I sit. Only a few minutes ago, when it was my route to this location from the beach, that extension of this rock was dry. I move a little higher up and watch the lower portion of the rock receive the brunt of the next wave. I'm in no danger here—my reading alerted me to folks being swept off rocks by errant waves, and I'm a cautious fellow—but I'll have to choose a different route when I leave the rocks. I watch the tide advance for a few minutes more.

When I feel spray reach this higher position where I'm sitting, I decide now might be a good time to go. The waves are too vigorous across the cobblestones. Instead, I scramble gingerly over the uneven surface atop the outcropping, then step carefully through that thicket of cairns—rather than topple any myself, I want to let storm tide decide their fate. Near the edge of the knob I pause to listen to the chatter of cobblestones a moment longer. I hope memory will record the sound, allow me to hear it again as I fall asleep tonight. Then I step onto the dry stones. The clatter of my crossing drowns out the sound of the cobblestones in the tide.

The trail rises again from the beach, veers easterly, and leads me around to high ground farther down the coast. When I reach an open bluff, I pause to look back and locate the spot where I listened to the cobblestones. Through binoculars I spot the cairn-adorned knob. It is now an island of rock; the cobblestone beach around it is completely submerged, and foaming waves are breaking on the cliff face beyond it. The sound of the cobblestones must be muted now, beneath the surf, but I know they will clatter again with the changing tide. What was simply a moment of attention for me is the timeless nature of their existence. Though few creatures hear it, the cobblestones have been making the same sounds, wearing themselves away slowly— slowly—by infinitesimal degrees, clattering, pinging, and clunking all the while, eons upon eons, open to change on every ebb and surge of the tide. My clattering across the cobblestones was only an instant of static in the ever-varying, timeless transmission of sound.

iv. Fog

An hour after sunrise, for which there is little evidence beyond the ability to see the fog better, I stand again on Schoodic Point. Last night, returning from a clear, sunny day on Mount Desert Island, I was surprised to find heavy fog cloaking the peninsula. The farther I drove, the more it thickened, until I could barely locate the beaches a

(Acadia National Park, Maine)

few yards beyond the shoulder of the road. Near the point Arey Cove was invisible behind an impenetrable white wall. Certain that the fog would still be here in the morning, I rose early, eager to get out into it.

I step slowly onto bare rock near the center of the point and at once detect motion down near the water's edge. Dozens of eiders waddle off the weed-smothered shore and plop into the ocean. I've only ever seen them floating offshore, never spotted them out of the water before. I raise the field glasses hanging around my neck and discover an immense flotilla stretching around the point, hundreds of little dark shapes imperturbably rising and settling with the waves. The farther out they bob, the more difficult they are to discern in the dense haze. From somewhere deep in the fog I hear a muted chugging, a lobster boat making its rounds; I shift my binoculars but only get a closer view of fog. On shore, in the rockweed just beyond the reach of the waves, a herring gull picks at a crab he's uncovered and dragged out of hiding. Early morning work for fishermen and gull.

I make my way toward the shore over the pink ledges and across two black dikes, searching for a gull guano–free zone somewhere close to the water. I find a narrow spot still unspotted and sit down on a low, narrow, nearly level block of stone. My feet rest on the slick algae of the black zone between rock untouchable by high tides and the sloping edge, where barnacles and green algae cling. The fog is thick and wet, the rock hard and cold; a familiar chill soon settles on me. The eiders, which were drifting eastward, begin drifting back west in a thin, widely spaced line; some them pop up out of the sea onto the tip of a nearby promontory and begin to probe the rockweed with their bills. The turning tide slams more vigorously against the shore. I sit with my pen poised above my daybook, but the chill makes my hand shake. The rest of me quivers at times as well.

Still, it's hard to leave. Having become one accustomed to the fog, I try to settle in. I've come here to be in the fog. I breathe in wet air, inhale deeply, and as I slowly exhale, I feel my senses open up to my surroundings. I gaze, I listen, I feel, I taste the fog. The waves slapping the rocks and splashing, gushing, rushing on every side, the gurgle and glug of water drawing out of the crevices around me, the silent thickening parade of eiders floating past, the ghostly shapes of a thin line of spruces against the inland fog behind me, rockweed on a low, nearly submerged ledge before me bearing the force of breakers and filtering the white foam—this turbulence and serenity together are ever changing and yet timeless. For how many millennia has it been like this? How long has this been going on? Being here, shivering in this precise moment, is like having been here at any moment in all those millennia. It's as if I could remember what the shore was like at the dawn of time because it's like that every minute, is like that now.

Only when I hear the occasional thrum of the lobster boat starting up again do I know for certain when the present moment is happening. Then it silences. Once more I become attuned to the rhythm of the waves, the white noise of the surf, the pulse of the tide. I can tell nothing about the world except for what I sense, what I see, hear, feel, breathe, exactly where I am, exactly now. I am simply alone—with the rocks, with the fog, with the tide—somewhere in time.

(Acadia National Park, Maine)

epilogue

Postscript to a Postscript to "The Ring of Time" (Sarasota, Florida)

> As I watched with the others, our jaws adroop, our eyes alight, I became painfully conscious of the element of time. Everything in the hideous old building seemed to take the shape of a circle, conforming to the course of the horse. The rider's gaze, as she peered straight ahead, seemed to be circular, as though bent by force of circumstance; then time itself began running in circles, and so the beginning was where the end was, and the two were the same, and one thing ran into the next and time went round and around and got nowhere. The girl wasn't so young that she did not know the delicious satisfaction of having a perfectly behaved body and the fun of using it to do a trick most people can't do, but she was too young to know that time does not really move in a circle at all. ... "She is at that enviable moment in life [I thought] when she believes she can go once around the ring, make one complete circuit, and at the end be exactly the same age as at the start."
>
> —E. B. WHITE, "The Ring of Time," *Essays of E. B. White*

At the start of my college teaching career, a considerable distance back in time, I happened to be teaching about myth and blundered onto one that had its origins in the South Pacific. It was the Myth of the Moon and the Banana. As I remember the story, it was an etiological myth, one that explained why some things are so in the world. At one point the gods, who had created man and woman and observed them with affection over the years, thought to grant them the gift of immortality—not the immortality of the gods, who were changeless and ageless throughout eternity, but, rather, an immortality appropriate to their human status. (I may be embellishing the story here, attributing motives to the gods; I think the version I originally read might have been simpler, less analytical about the rationale for the choices the gods gave the first couple.) The first man and the first woman were invited to choose between two kinds of immortality, the immortality of the moon or the immortality of the banana.

The moon's immortality is cyclical. It waxes from nothing into radiant fullness, then wanes into nothingness, then reemerges from blackness again and so on, in perpetuity. The banana's immortality is generational. It comes from sending out, season after season, new shoots that emerge from the shoots of the season before. Sometimes I asked my students to choose one of these two immortalities for themselves; sometimes I asked them to tell me which one the first couple chose and why we know they chose it.

But by the time I first encountered this myth and taught it, I was the father of a three-year-old son and a one-year-old daughter, and I knew what distinguished the choices. The immortality of the moon is immortality through the eternal death and resurrection of the self, reincarnation from a certain form back into the same form over and over again. It's a selfish immortality. The immortality of the banana is immortality through the reproduction of progeny, passing on your essence into new life forms that take your place in the world at the cost of your withering and wasting and passing out of the world. It's a generous immortality.

The first couple chose the immortality of the banana, and ever since, human beings have children, and their children have children, and each generation replaces itself with a new generation that eventually will be replaced by another in its turn.

I was a father; I had a son and a daughter in the world. I told my students that the first couple had made the right choice. It seemed like the obvious choice to make.

Near the end of my college teaching career—not at the exact end but close enough to it that I might have been able to see the end if I'd realized it was coming—I wrote a book about E. B. White's career as an essayist. My first significant encounter with White's essays had been, again, at the start of that career, when, as the new father of a son, I had read "Once More to the Lake." The essay was about White's spending time with his son at a camp in Maine at which he himself had spent many summer vacations with his own father. Throughout the essay White claims to be confused about who he is at the camp, the father or the son, because it seems to him that the camp is unchanging, timeless, as if no time had passed between his visits *as son*, with his father, and his visit *as father*, with his son. But in the end he watches as his son takes a wet swimsuit from a clothesline and pulls up "around his vitals the small, soggy, icy garment." He writes, "As he buckled the swollen belt suddenly my groin felt the chill of death." It's an acknowledgment that, in spite of his repeated assertion that "there had been no years," time has indeed passed— his own father is gone, and he in turn will leave behind his own son.

When I read that passage for the first time, I wept, suddenly aware of my own mortality prefigured in the life of my son, as if I had willingly begun to expend myself in order to achieve his existence. It seemed a perfectly acceptable exchange.

This had been the theme of White's great essay, and by the time I was nearing the end of my career, I wrote the book because I wanted to know why White had never equaled that great essay in the voluminous course of all his other writing. In the end I believed that "Once More to the Lake" was the one essay that drew upon the whole span of his life—in a sense, unlike his other writing, he had been writing this essay for thirty-seven years.

I didn't know then that an essayist may only get one chance to write such an essay; I only learned that by trying to write *this* essay. And I have to get this essay right *this* time, because it will likely be the only chance I get.

Florida is hard for me to imagine. I live in a temperate zone year round, one occasionally intemperate only when lake-effect blizzards gust across the landscape, and except for a few years in Iowa, I've never lived far from the Canadian border. I think of four seasons cycling through the years as the way of the world, take particular pleasure in the transitions of the moderate seasons, endure—*almost* ungrudgingly—the brief intensities of the extreme seasons. Nothing in my northern life prepared me for Florida.

We began traveling to Florida when Caroline, our youngest, moved to Sarasota after graduation from Penn State. We fly into Tampa, usually on the weekend when Sue's spring break ends and mine begins, end of February or start of March, from deep in the northern winter, and stride through the airport's air-conditioned chill, then gasp as our lungs take in the first blast of moist air when we step outside. Somehow we are never prepared for that first moment of instantaneous wilting. The air is heavy, humid, fecund, and thick. The unfamiliar foliage—the towering palm trees and squat succulent shrubs—seems like stage scenery, a cliché of tropical décor.

We drive off toward the Gulf of Mexico, cross the mouth of Tampa Bay, and curl inland to join the interstate south to Sarasota. Pelicans glide like unflappable pterodactyls just offshore, and cormorants dry themselves on pilings and channel markers, and often we spot an egret stalking the shallows. The piers and buoys are modern, but the birds have been part of the landscape since Florida rose from the ocean. Crossing the bay on the Sunshine State Parkway, we rise toward the zenith of the bridge, its tension wires arranged like a sail sculpture across the hump, and momentarily lose sight of the land, seem to be heading into an expansive blue sky and leaving the earth altogether. Then we cross the apex of the bridge and plummet toward a low, lush landscape that seems to keep its head above water entirely by inadvertence rather than design. Somehow, after years of visiting Caroline, all of this should be familiar, but instead of déjà vu, we always have the feeling we are seeing it for the first time, or like the weatherman played by Bill Murray in *Groundhog Day*, seeing it for the first time again and again.

When Caroline moved to Sarasota with a degree in art and journalism, she took a job in a photo retail store, thinking it would keep her connected to the photography she'd concentrated on. But the store was sold to a chain, which streamlined and cheapened the operation, and she quit, falling back on waitressing, the line of work she'd learned at Ye Olde College Diner. It was on an occasion when she was trying to list for me all the places she'd worked, the series of restaurants that she'd left when they had closed or been sold to more difficult or less competent new owners, that she complained about time in Florida.

"There's no way to keep track of time here," she said. "It's all the same time. Everyday is like every other day."

For someone raised around the Great Lakes, in the land of four seasons, the quotidian tropical life along the Gulf of Mexico seems static and seasonless. How can you keep track of time when it's always summer and no winter, spring, or fall ever jostles your awareness of passing time?

E. B. White also went regularly from his home in Maine to Sarasota, for a winter respite, exchanging, as he put it, "the land of the fir tree and pine" for "the land of the palm tree and vine." His earliest essay on the Gulf Coast was "On a Florida Key," written in February 1941; his last was "What Do Our Hearts Treasure?" written in January 1966. In between, on March 22, 1956, he wrote his second-best-known essay, "The Ring of Time." It is in that essay that he describes the teenage bareback rider practicing her circles in the circus tent and imagines her thinking that time is standing still; in the second part of the essay he brings up the southern resistance to racial integration and suggests that time is not standing still at all. At the end of the essay he observes that "there is certainly a great temptation in Florida to duck the passage of time. Lying in warm comfort by the sea, you receive gratefully the gift of the sun, the gift of the South. This is true seduction. The day is a circle—morning, afternoon, and night. After a few days I was clearly enjoying the same delusion as the girl on the horse—that I could ride clear around the ring of day, guarded by wind and sun and sea and sand, and be not a moment older." He may enjoy the delusion, but he is fully aware that it is a delusion.

"The Ring of Time" was first published in the *New Yorker* and then reprinted in White's collection *The Points of My Compass* with a postscript dated April 1962. The postscripts were ways of bringing what might have seemed, to a weekly journalist, outdated material down to date, and in this p.s. White mentions changes to what he calls Fiddler Bayou since his earliest visits, when "it was wild land, populated chiefly by the little crabs that gave it its name," and since his visit to the Ringling circus winter headquarters six years earlier. The changes involve the relocating of the circus and the development of the land and the quickening of the pace of life. He observes, "Time has not stood still for anybody but the dead, and even the dead must be able to hear the acceleration of the sports cars and know that things have changed."

The reckless, impulsive pursuit of change plagued him, and his letters from the South seldom fail to refer to it. In a letter to his brother Stanley datelined "Siesta Key, Sarasota, Fla 5 March 1960" White observed that "Florida real estate is just as delirious as ever" and described the digging of channels to make "every piece of property a 'water front' piece," which he felt was "as practical as the Paris sewers and just about as pleasing to the eye." On St. Valentine's Day 1963 he wrote Stanley, "I'm sitting right in the middle of one of the better population explosions, and I have green memories of what this delectable sandbar was like before the fuse was touched off. The city fathers of Sarasota regard themselves as visionaries if they look as far ahead as, say, nineteen days. Anything beyond that is too far in the future to be worth monkeying with." His scorn was particularly directed in this letter at dredging to enlarge real estate holdings at Bird Key and the resulting erosion along the beaches and subsequent construction of groins to stop the erosion, "so that what was once a lovely little stretch of natural beach, complete with dunes, sea grape, and Australian pine, now looks like a broken-down docking facility." In March 1968 he wrote Edward Weeks, "Katharine and I are sitting out the winter on our favorite sandbar, watching the Gulf of Mexico quietly disappear behind the high-rise buildings." His letter to David Dodd dated 13 February 1972 lamented, "If Sarasota had had a modicum of intensive care about thirty or forty years ago, it might be a far fairer city today—and the fishing might be better, too. I miss the early times of Fiddler Bayou, the years when K and I occupied the Achterlonie house and really enjoyed ourselves. There were no condominiums, and everybody had plenty of time of day. And when the sun failed to shine, we lay peacefully listening to the rain." In the letters he is less accepting of the passage of time, more begrudging of the encroachment of change, and he seems less inclined to be deluded by the illusion of timelessness in Florida's climate.

It took me awhile after Caroline moved to Sarasota to remember that E. B. White had repeatedly vacationed there, but when I did, I sent her photocopies of his Florida essays and letters. I began to think that the next time I went to Sarasota to visit her I ought to explore the places White stayed, if they still existed, in order to write something that would be a postscript to his postscript to "The Ring of Time" as well as a postscript to my own book about his writing.

Caroline herself reinforced that idea by locating a house in the return address of some of the letters. It turned out that she knew someone whose mother was renting the house; apparently, other writers had rented it as well as White, but she didn't know who. The next time we traveled south, she drove us past the address, but the high fence along the road and the angled driveway made it difficult to see the house, and the traffic was so fast and heavy that we didn't dare slow down rounding the curve. Caroline's friend's mother had been told by the woman who owns the house that she used to keep blankets near the fence, to cover the bodies from the car wrecks that happened on that curve.

I thought a lot about that house afterward, imagined poking around in it and maybe hearing tales of White's tenancy from the owner, but in the end I didn't ask Caroline if she could arrange a tour. In the North or on the plane coming or going, it seems like a good idea, but when I'm in Sarasota, I think about how seldom I see my daughter and how short a time we'll have on our visit, and it feels too much like squandering my time with her to set off on a research excursion.

Besides, in Florida it seems as if time doesn't pass at all, and nothing's changed in the year between our visits, and I have all the time in the world to get this done if I want to.

If you return to the same place at the same time of year over and over, it becomes difficult to distinguish one visit from another—was that the time we went to the Marie Selby Botanical Garden? was that the time we kayaked off of Longboat Key? did we eat at Columbo's that time, or was it the Café L'Europe? Even if I jot down a quick overview of our activities in my journal, it is the moments that stay in my memory, not the sense of time. The moments could have happened on any trip.

On one visit—it could have been any visit—we drive out from the mainland to Longboat Key, where we have reservations with Mote Marine Aquarium for a boat tour of Sarasota and Roberts Bays. We cruise in the bright sunshine for a couple of hours. A dolphin rises near the boat once or twice, a flash of dark back and dorsal fin, then submerges and veers away from our course. An osprey perched on a piling with a fish in its talons flies off at our approach. We slowly circle a couple of red mangrove islands densely populated with rookeries for great blue herons, great egrets, snowy egrets, double-crested cormorants, and pelicans. The birds preen and bustle and intimidate one another, their croaks and squawks warning us and each other away. We disembark on Big Edwards Island, one of two islands formed by dredging, mostly to identify two pest trees imported from other countries, the Brazilian peppertree and the Australian pine. As we head back to the aquarium, the biologist on the boat trolls for fish with a dragnet, brings up a variety of local denizens to display— puffer fish, flounder, pinfish, blue crab, spider crab, several more. By the time we reach the shore again, we feel we have a better sense of where we are.

The following morning we take a two-hour walk on the beach on Siesta Key, a long flat stretch of white seashell sand open to the Gulf of Mexico and paralleled back of the beach grass and low dunes by resorts and hotels and condominiums. We walk this beach each time we come. Others walk it or run it too, usually retired couples, senior citizens, women in pairs or groups. No one stays in our memories, and for however many years we've annually walked this beach, we have no idea whether we've passed the same people on two different occasions. We sometimes swim but mostly simply stroll or stride. This morning foot traffic is light—perhaps it is too early in the day— and we notice Caspian terns, sandpipers, laughing gulls, plovers, and pelicans in profusion. When we glance offshore, we see a pod of half a dozen dolphins, barely arcing out of and into the water parallel with us. Three more emerge briefly farther out. We look around, but no one else is close to us, no one else is sharing this moment. It is the only time we see dolphins offshore.

That afternoon we drive inland fourteen miles to Myakka River State Park, notable for its Florida dry prairie terrain, its alligators, and its birds. Along the shores of Upper Myakka Lake, we amble along a bird walk ramp extending out into the marshes and spot a wonderful panoply of shorebirds, most of them exotic finds for us: common moorhen, glossy ibis, American coot, blue-winged teal, great blue heron, great egret, snowy egret, little blue heron, Louisiana or tricolored heron, phoebes, yellow-rumped warblers, mottled ducks, mockingbirds, snipes. Alligators occasionally float ominously past. After we leave the bird walk, we hike in the heat of the afternoon about five miles over inland trails, taking in the open stretches of rare dry prairie and shady hammocks of live oak. In the heat of midday we see none of the birds that thrive in the prairie, but we get glimpses of natural past, sense the illusion of timelessness.

February 10, 2001, the hand of time moves before my eyes.

For Caroline's wedding we intend to fly to Miami, rent a car, stay overnight in a motel, then drive to Key West, where the ceremony will take place. In Detroit our flight changes terminals and departure gates without warning, and after all passengers board, we all have to disembark and wait for another plane at another gate; instead of reaching Miami at midnight, we are scheduled to arrive at two thirty in the morning. Weary from a long day of preparation and planning and unpredictable travel problems, jumpy during a bumpy flight, I don't write on the plane and don't even try to read. I sit with my overhead light off, hoping to nap, my mind restless and filled with images of my daughter over the years.

A favorite memory of her as a baby has stayed with me and filled me with longing throughout her lifetime. When she and her mother and brother and I moved to Michigan, where I was starting my university teaching career, she was about to turn one year old; we celebrated her first birthday in a townhouse near the university, a few days after Labor Day, when we moved in. Two months later we bought a house a few blocks away, still an easy walk to my office, and we moved again. That first year of teaching I taught four classes on Monday, Wednesday, and Friday, the first one at eight o'clock in the morning. My office mate taught at the same time. Around seven thirty he would stroll up to my house from a faculty rental in university housing at the end of my street, and we would walk to work together, down to the end of a side street, along a short path and over a little creek, and through the parking lot.

When I awoke each morning, my wife would stay in bed, and I would go into the bathroom with my clothes, shave and shower and dress, and come out to make my breakfast. Tom had the large bedroom opposite ours, and Caroline's room was next to his, opposite the bathroom. It was a simple ranch style house, and the dining area was at the end of the kitchen, with patio doors leading to a deck and a backyard that looked out on the tower dormitories of the university. That first year Caroline learned how to climb out of her crib, and most mornings I would open the bathroom door to find her sitting in the hallway, waiting in the dark for me to come out. I would lift my little girl into my arms, and we would welcome the day together.

I would quietly take her back into her room, change her, and then take her into the kitchen with me, making her breakfast as well as my own. By the time John was at the door to start our short trek to school, I would have cleaned her up and taken her into my bedroom, to put her to bed with her mother. I'd had precious time with Tom when I was a graduate student, a stay-at-home father for half of each day; this was my time with Caroline, never long enough but precious all the same.

Not long after Caroline turned three, her mother and I separated, and I moved out, and my time with her and Tom shifted to the weekends, and everything was different.

Often in my life I have felt a palpable ache, a sensation in my arms and chest, from longing to hold that baby in my arms again. Maybe I would feel that way even if her mother and I hadn't divorced, but maybe it comes from a sense of irretrievable loss from not having been with my children each day. When you are a divorced parent, it's not enough to rebuild your life and find your own happiness with another partner; you may feel blessed and grateful, a recipient of unmerited grace, but a part of you is always holding your breath, longing for certain signs of your children's happiness, irrefutable indications that anguish is no longer waiting in the wings just out of your peripheral vision. Sharing your daughter's joy at her wedding might be just such a sign; just because you had to marry twice to find your contentment is no reason to believe she hasn't gotten it right the first time. Exhale all the way for once. For once, on faith, stop holding your breath.

Caroline, the youngest of the three children in our blended family, is the first to marry. Among my siblings I had been the last to marry and far and away the last to have children; my children are much younger than most of their cousins, and the first wedding we attended together was the wedding of my brother's younger daughter, Karen. At the reception at the Knights of Columbus Hall in my hometown, I saw again relatives I hadn't seen for years and was sometimes startled to see how they'd aged. But the biggest surprise was to watch my brother David, six years younger than I, performing as the father of the bride, the guy in charge of things whom the caterers conferred with, the guy dancing with his daughter in her long flowing white bridal gown and veil. Our own father and stepmother sat off to one side with relatives of their generation, chatting and joking; it seemed not that long ago my father was giving my sisters away at their weddings, was the groom in his own second wedding. At my niece's wedding I danced for the first time with Caroline, for the first time with Becky, a father dancing with his daughters. When the disc jockey worked his way back in time to Glenn Miller and Tommy Dorsey recordings, it was my sister Linda and I who jitterbugged on the dance floor—people actually cleared the floor for us as we took on roles that had always been those of my mother and my uncle Gene. It was like a ritual of transition in swingtime, torches passing from one generation to another—now we are the parents and uncles and aunts, and our children are the brides and grooms. I thought: I have to remember this moment.

In the plane on the way to my daughter's wedding I do remember that moment, and I think: And now I am the father of the bride. The ceremony won't be very formal—it will be performed on a restored nineteenth-century schooner sailing at sunset on the Gulf of Mexico, and the ship's captain will officiate—and my role is chiefly to stand by beaming with love, but I am still the father of the bride. And I remember my brother as the father of the bride and remember thinking at my niece's wedding that on your wedding day you ought to be allowed to feel that you are the center of the universe, that all of creation approves of your joy. It was a thought I'd had at weddings before, and I will think it again, joyfully, at my daughter's wedding and remember its companion thought, that you really get to share feeling like the center of the universe on your wedding day—that the only day you actually occupy the center alone is the day you're born, a day you don't remember and can't appreciate. You deserve to have that feeling on your wedding day.

For this flight to Florida, for once, I haven't packed the E. B. White folder, but I think about the unwritten essay, almost reflexively, as I drowse on the plane. Suddenly awareness sweeps over me like a blush. I think: I haven't been able to write the essay because it isn't about Florida and E. B. White and time; it's about time and my daughter and me. It's only an illusion that time hasn't been passing, that we haven't aged an instant when we complete the circuit around the ring. The moment commemorates the change, but the change has been in progress all along, in infinitesimal increments building to this ceremonial culmination. We feel we have been occupying the same position in the family portrait and suddenly discover that we're somewhere else, as if we've been moving without realizing it—as if the ground beneath our feet has been shifting our location while we've been preoccupied trying to stand still for the photographer.

September 2003. One morning, as I drag myself out of bed, I hear an interview on the radio with a woman whose father was a victim of snipers last year, and in spite of the fact that everything about their lives differed from ours, I still felt an electric current of recognition run through me. I remember it is my father's birthday from not seeing it marked on the calendar, as his and my father-in-law's had both been recorded for so many Septembers before, and I am suddenly aware of another way to notice the passage of time. My father died in January 2002; my granddaughter was born at the end of July 2003. For the rest of the day my recurring mantra is: My father is no longer in the world, and Zola is now in the world.

Less than two months ago, when we met Zola soon after her birth, my son Tom, now also a resident of Florida, asked me how I felt to be a grandfather. I felt stunned with wonder—again, as I'd felt at his birth and at his sister's birth—but I also felt as if I'd been happily moved farther down the pecking order of life. It's a splendid part of aging, this discovery that your child's child is the new center of the universe. I told Tom my center of the universe theory about births and weddings and expanded it by explaining that on the day of your child's birth you are aware that you've lost center status, that you've been relegated to a supporting role and that your child has assumed center status. Grandparents, on that same day, shift into cameo character roles. It may be a demotion, but it feels very like a lifetime achievement award.

Soon Sue and I, taking advantage of some unexpected work travel for her and a long weekend for me, will go to Sarasota again, see Caroline, Tim, and Zola, and be joined by Tom, who'll drive down from Orlando. Tom will be freshly back from a trip to Alaska, where he touched down in the forty-ninth state he's been to as a way of celebrating his thirtieth birthday. A week and a day later Zola will be two months old.

So here's the passage of time for you—or at least for me. Thirty years ago, just as my father turned 52, less than two years after my mother died at 48, my son was born. This year, as I prepare to turn 61, less than two years after my father died at 80, just after my daughter turns 28 and my son turns 30, my granddaughter completes only her second month of life. I think about her every day, and I wish my father could know that she's in the world, just as I wished my mother could have known about my children being in the world. My children grew up distant from their grandparents and step-grandparents, almost all of whom are out of the world now, which means that their children will never know great-grandparents (neither did I for that matter, though some of them lived into my childhood). When Zola is her mother's age, I'll be 88; when she's Tom's age, I'll be 90 (Tom says that, with advances in medicine, I could go to 125, a daunting prospect). Odds are that I will never meet my own great-grandchildren.

I don't think these are gloomy thoughts, just random reflections on the very real passage of time. We don't measure it in the passage of days; here in Michigan this morning was colder than yesterday morning, and we turned on the heat for only the second or third time since June, but we do not feel a shifting of time, and in Florida, where heat and humidity are relatively constant, it's even harder to differentiate the days. We really measure time in the contrast of events in our lives. Zola's birth moves me into an outer ring one more remove from the center of the universe, and at the next remove I will likely drop out of the world or at least have very little time at that station before I do. Zola, starting from scratch, has so much to learn, is just learning how to learn about the world. Her uncle Tom, who has seen London and Lisbon and Japan, who has been to every state except Hawai'i, has seen much in his thirty years; her aunt Becky, who has lived in California and Chicago, who has worked with autistic children and works in a neonatal unit, has seen much in her thirty-two years. Zola's universe now is so enclosed, from her mother's womb to her parents' arms and the apartment on Osprey Avenue and the few neighborhood blocks where they push her stroller. She has so much universe to expand into, to explore.

Honey, I want to say to her, you're so tiny and the world is so big, and what a good start you've had on being in the world. How much better the world seems to me for your being in it, and as much as I want to be in your world for as long as I can, how much more prepared, more accepting I am, of leaving it, now that I know it's yours.

Time is not a circle. Time is not a ring. You can't go once around the ring and be the same age at the end as at the beginning. Time is a spiral, and its scale is such that we see so little of it, and it seems we are traveling in circles. We speak of the cycle of the days, the cycle of the seasons, the phases of the moon, sunrise, sunset, swiftly flow the days, as if these were simple unchanging repetitions, and only a strictly meteorological approach to each day records the slightly later or earlier sunrise, the slightly later or earlier sunset, the progress of the planet around the sun. We can intellectually apprehend the geologic scale of time, the historic scale of time, but we can no more experience them than a dust mote or a grain of sand can experience the scale of the Grand Canyon—what sedimentation? what erosion? Take your place on the great mandala, the wheel of time rolling across existence; however long your life in days and years, it will be infinitesimally short in the scale of time, the duration of the wheel's passage through the intersection between eternity and entity.

(Sarasota, Florida)

Time is a spiral, a corkscrew. The son walking with his father by the lake becomes the father walking with his son by the lake, and that son will one day be a father walking with his son by the lake. The girl riding bareback around the ring while her mother guides the horse will one day be the mother guiding the horse while her daughter rides bareback around the ring. We have been granted not the immortality of the moon but the immortality of the banana. What a blessing to be able to measure time this way.

select bibliography

The Pattern of Life Indelible

Elledge, Scott. *E. B. White: A Biography*. New York: Norton, 1984.

White, E. B. *Essays of E. B. White*. New York: Harper & Row, 1977.

———. *Letters of E. B. White*. Ed. Dorothy Lobrano Guth. New York: Harper & Row, 1976.

———. *One Man's Meat*. New York: Harper & Row, 1982.

The Everlastingly Great Look of the Sky

Thoreau, Henry David. *Walden*. Ed. J. Lyndon Shanley. Princeton: Princeton University Press, 1971.

White, E. B. *Letters of E. B. White*. Ed. Dorothy Lobrano Guth. New York: Harper & Row, 1976.

———. "A Slight Sound at Evening." *Essays of E. B. White*, 234–42. New York: Harper & Row, 1977

———. "Walden." *One Man's Meat*, 65–70. New York: Harper & Row, 1982.

Whitman, Walt. *Prose Works 1892*. Vol. 1: *Specimen Days*. Ed. Floyd Stovall. New York: New York University Press, 1963.

Here Is New York

White, E. B. *Here Is New York*. New York: Harper & Brothers, 1949.

Knowing Where You've Been

Maclean, Norman. "USFS 1919: The Logger, the Cook, and the Hole in the Sky." *A River Runs Through It and Other Stories*. Chicago: University of Chicago Press, 1979.

Of Trees and Time

Allman, Laurie. "Warren Woods, April," *Far From Tame: Reflections from the Heart of a Continent*. Minneapolis: University of Minnesota Press, 1996.

Malabar Farm

Anderson, David D. "Louis Bromfield, Nature Writer and Practical Ecologist," *Ohio: In Fact and Fiction: Further Essays on the Ohio Experience.*

East Lansing: Midwestern Press, Center for the Study of Midwestern Literature and Culture, 2006: 134–41.

Berry, Wendell. "The Necessity of Agriculture," *Harper's Magazine* (December 2009): 15–16. Originally delivered May 16, 2009, at Malabar Farm.

Bromfield, Louis. *Louis Bromfield at Malabar: Writings of Farming and Country Life*. Ed. Charles E. Little. Baltimore: Johns Hopkins University Press, 1988.

White, E. B. "Book Review ("Malabar Farm" by Louis Bromfield)," *The Second Tree From the Corner* (New York: Harper & Brothers, 1954: 144–48. First published in *The New Yorker* (May 8, 1948).

White, E. B. *Letters of E. B. White*. New York: Harper & Row, 1976: 243.

Wilson, Edmund. "What Became of Louis Bromfield," *Classics and Commercials: A Literary Chronicle of the Forties*. New York: Farrar, Straus, 1947: 153–60. First published in *The New Yorker* (April 1, 1944).

Terra Cognita

Belanger, Pamela J. *Inventing Acadia: Artists and Tourists at Mount Desert*. Rockland ME: Farnsworth Art Museum, 1999.

Time and Tide

Carson, Rachel. *The Edge of the Sea*. New York: Houghton Mifflin, 1955.
Fox, William T. *At the Sea's Edge: An Introduction to Coastal Oceanography for the Amateur Naturalist*. Englewood Cliffs NJ: Prentice-Hall, 1983.
Hurd, Barbara, "Fine Distinctions." *Fourth Genre: Explorations in Nonfiction* 8:2 (Fall 2006): 1–10. Reprinted as "Pebbles: Fine Distinctions." *Walking the Wrackline: On Tidal Shifts and What Remains*. Athens: University of Georgia Press, 2008.

Postscript to a Postscript to "The Ring of Time"

White, E. B. *Essays of E. B. White*. New York: Harper & Row, 1977.
———. *Letters of E. B. White*. Ed. Dorothy Lobrano Guth. New York: Harper & Row, 1976.

Also by Robert Root

As Author—

Following Isabella: Travels in Colorado Then and Now (2009)

The Nonfictionist's Guide: On Reading and Writing Nonfiction (2007)

Recovering Ruth: A Biographer's Tale (2003)

E. B. White: The Emergence of an Essayist (1999)

Wordsmithery: A Guide to Working at Writing (1994, 1998)

Working at Writing: Columnists and Critics Composing (1991)

The Rhetorics of Popular Culture: Advertising, Advocacy, Entertainment (1987)

Thomas Southerne (1981)

As Editor—

Landscapes with Figures: The Nonfiction of Place (2007)

Diaries of an Isle Royale Fisherman by Elling A. Seglem (with Jill Burkland, 2002)

The Island within Us: Isle Royale Artists-in-Residence, 1991–1998 (with Jill Burkland, 2000)

The Fourth Genre: Contemporary Writers of/on Creative Nonfiction (with Michael Steinberg, 1999, 2002, 2005, 2007, 2009, 2012)

"Time By Moments Steals Away": The 1848 Journal of Ruth Douglass (1998)

Those Who Do, Can: Teachers Writing, Writers Teaching (with Michael Steinberg, 1996)

Critical Essays on E. B. White (1994)